Giuseppe Levi

Il maestro d'inglese

Nuovo metodo facile e pratico

Giuseppe Levi

Il maestro d'inglese
Nuovo metodo facile e pratico

ISBN/EAN: 9783741143953

Manufactured in Europe, USA, Canada, Australia, Japa

Cover: Foto ©Andreas Hilbeck / pixelio.de

Manufactured and distributed by brebook publishing software (www.brebook.com)

Giuseppe Levi

Il maestro d'inglese

IL

MAESTRO D'INGLESE

NUOVO METODO FACILE E PRATICO

PEL

DOTT. GIUSEPPE LEVI

Professore patentato e già pubblico insegnante.

PARTE SECONDA
Sintassi — Fraseologia — Epistolario.

FIRENZE
DALLA TIPOGRAFIA CENNINIANA
nelle Murate, Via Ghibellina 8
—
1870

AVVERTENZA

Questa seconda parte tratterà più specialmente della sintassi; però il nostro metodo essendo molto più pratico che teorico, ci premeva colla prima parte mettere l'allievo in grado di leggere un libro coll'aiuto del dizionario, acciò meno noioso gli riesca lo studio della lingua; e però alcune delle regole grammaticali di un uso pratico meno frequente dovevano naturalmente trovar qui il loro posto; così pure è nella seconda parte che molte eccezioni devono essere indicate.

Per ciò che riguarda la pronuncia, ci parrebbe puerile continuare a segnarla come abbiamo fatto nella prima parte. In una lezione preliminare daremo la teoria dell'accentuazione, e metteremo sotto gli occhi dell'allievo una tabella delle abbreviazioni tanto in uso presso gl'Inglesi. Affine di richiamare le regole, andremo di quando in quando, segnando sopra la parola il numero romano, non tralasciando di dare il più chiaramente possibile la pronuncia delle parole più strane; confidando del resto che l'orecchio che l'allievo deve necessariamente aver formato e la conoscenza teoretica che deve possedere, ci esonerino da più oltre segnare la pronuncia ad ogni parola nuova che saremo per indicare; finalmente, ogni qual volta ci si offrirà il destro, faremo sulla pronuncia tutte quelle osservazioni che crederemo opportune e che serviranno a rendere completissimo l'insegnamento teorico-pratico della pronuncia inglese.

Ci piace pure notare, che comunque anche in questa seconda parte la pratica occupi un posto maggiore della teoria, tuttavia abbiamo creduto conveniente sviluppare tutta la teoria della lingua, e disporre le lezioni in modo che di essa teoria l'allievo se ne faccia un'idea chiarissima; a questa sola condizione, arrivato alla fine del nostro libro uno potrà dire di conoscere la lingua inglese.

LEZIONE PRELIMINARE
DELL'ACCENTUAZIONE E ABBREVIAZIONE.

Le parole o sono derivate o radicali:

A — Quando una parola è DERIVATA, qualunque sia il numero delle sillabe che vi sono aggiunte l'ACCENTO si trova sulla parola RADICALE.
Es.: *Friend—friend-ship—friend-ly—un-friend-ly—un-friend-li-ness.*

B — Vi sono molte parole che servono per nome e verbo, e talvolta anche aggettivo; quando è nome ovvero aggettivo l'ACCENTO cade sulla *prima sillaba*, e quando è *verbo* sull'*ultima*.
Es.: *prés-ent* (regalo), *pris-ent* (presente), *to present* (offrire, regalare; insult (insulto), to insult (insultare), object (oggetto), to object (obbiettare).*

C — Nelle parole di DUE SILLABE l'accento cade:
Sulla **prima** quando la parola finisce con una sola consonante: — Es.: *pá-per, ma-rket.*
Ed ancora se finisce con { *age — ice — ive — ure — ard -ing—ish—ck—le—nce—nt -y—our—ow—cy* }
Es.: *cóur-age, práe-tice, ácti-ve,* (*) *si-lence, fríi-guent, hán-py, hón-our. fól-low, má-ney.*

Sull'**ultima**: 1° quando la parola finisce con una *sola consonante* ed è finale.
2° quando finisce con *più consonanti* tranne *ard, ing, ish, ck, nt, o con y*).
3° quando trovasi nell'*ultima* sillaba *un dittongo* tranne *our, ow, oey*).
Es.: *dispúte.*
Es.: *remárk.*
Es.: *re-máin.*

D — La **vocale** od il *dittongo* innanzi alle desinenze IAL, TAL, ION, IOUS, UOUS, IC ITY, ha sempre l'ACCENTO, abbia la parola 3, 4, 5, o 6 sillabe. L'ACCENTO si trova sempre sull'A nella desinenza *ator* tranne in *conspirator*).

E — Nelle parole di TRE SILLABE l'ACCENTO cade:
Sulla **prima**, quando sono primitive (regola generale) Es.: *gén-er-al*
Sulla **seconda** nelle parole *primitive* seguenti: — *ac-cóm-plish, aban-dos, ad-ja-cent, ab-ól-ish, ad-món-ish,* etc.
Sull'**ultima** quando sono derivate direttamente dal francese e che hanno le desinenze *ade, ee, ier*: — *promenáde, gren-ad-iér,* ed in molte altre.

(*) Per le parole che finiscono in *ice (v. ice),* si osservi che l'*i* non avendo sopra di sè l'accento, per la presente regola, esso non si pronunzia secondo il suono alfabetico, ma avrà il suono breve cioè simile all'italiano.

Per ciò che riguarda le parole di quattro, cinque o sei sillabe, siccome per la maggior parte sono derivate, si osserverà la regola qui sopra, le altre poche che non sono derivate saranno annotate all'occasione che si presenteranno.

TAVOLA DELLE ABBREVIAZIONI (*).

Althò', *invece di* althòugh.		ne'ér, *invece di* nèver.	
àn't (v.),	am not.	ó',	of, on.
àrn't (v.),	are not.	ó'er,	òver.
Bàrt.,	Bàronet.	òn't,	on it.
by't.	by it.	ò'th' (v.),	of the.
càn't,	cànnot.	're,	àre.
couldn't,	could not.	'rt,	àrt.
'd,	would, had.	shàn't (v),	shàll not.
d'yó,	do you.	shé'd,	she would, she had.
dòn't,	do not.		
do't (v.),	do it.	shé's,	she is.
e'er,	èver.	shou'dn't,	should not.
e'én,	éven.	th',	the.
'èm (v.),	them.	thàt's,	that is.
Esq.,	Esquíre	thère's,	thère is.
fòr't,	for it.	they're,	they are.
hàdn't,	hàd nòt.	they'd,	they would, they
hàve n't,	have not.	they'll,	they will. (had)
bé'd,	he had.	t'other (v.),	the other.
hé'd,	he would.	thò',	thòugh.
hé'll (**),	he will	thou'dst,	thou wouldst.
hè's,	he is	thou'lt,	thou wilt.
'gainst,	against.	thou'rt,	thou art.
hére's,	hére is.	thou'st,	thou hast.
Hòn.,	*H*ònorable.	tà'en,	taken.
i'd.,	I had.	'twère,	it wère.
i'd.,	I would.	'tis,	it is.
I'll (**),	I will.	'tisn't,	it is not.

(*) Quelle notate (v) vengono adoperate soltanto dal volgo.
(**) *Will* si può abbreviare quando è segno del futuro semplice, ma non quando significa *volere*.

I'll, *invece di*	I shall.	(viz.) vidèlicet, námely (*).	
I'm,	I am.	wasn't (v.),	was not.
in't,	in it.	wé'd,	we had.
i'the (v.),	in the.	wé'd,	we would.
i've,	I have.	wé're,	we are.
is n't'	is not.	wèren't,	were not.
it's,	it is.	wé've,	we have.
i é,	id est, that is.	what's,	what is.
lèt'em (v.),	lèt them.	whère's,	whère is.
lèt'es	let us.	who's,	who is.
mùst n't,	mùst not.	wòn't,	will not.
Mà'am,	Màdàm	wou'dn't,	would not.
màyn't (v.),	mày not	you'd,	you had.
mightn't,	might not.	you'll,	you will.
Mèssrs.,	Mèssieurs	you're,	you are.
Mr.	Mister.	you,ve,	you have.
Mrs.,	Mistres.		

(*) *Namely* significa *cioè*, nello scrivere si usa l'abbreviativo latino *viz*, però si deve pronunciare *namely*.

Lezione trentesima quinta.　　　Lesson the thirty fifth.

SINTASSI E PARTICOLARITÀ DELL' ARTICOLO.

263.

Non si deve confondere l'articolo indeterminato *a an* col numero *one*, quest'ultimo si userà quando si vuol indicare l'unità e non più; p. e.:

I want one horse not two, Ho bisogno d'un cavallo non di due.

Gli articoli, tanto il determinato che l'indeterminato si mettono dopo le parole *half,* mezzo, *such,* tale, *what!* che!

I nomi che esprimono la patria, la professione, la qualità di una persona vogliono esser preceduti dall'articolo indeterminato, p. e.

　　　　　he is a German, egli è tedesco

dear me! povero me!

talented, d'ingegno　　　　*blockhead,* stupido

pupil, allievo　　　　　　*milliner,* modista

A man could do such a thing but not a woman. One talented man could do it, but ten blockheads could not. Dear me, what a blockhead you are; you never understand what I tell you. I have given him half a dozen useful books for a watch which is good for nothing. Have you a pupil named Francis? I have two, but one is a talented boy, the other is such a blockhead that will never learn any thing. What is his father? I think he is a merchant. You mistake he is a painter. What is his country? He is a German and his wife is an Italian. What a beautiful woman! Do you know her? Yes she is a milliner. Do you know her husband? She is a widow. Dear me, what an ugly dog you have brought home! It is your physician's. Where have you been so long? I beg your pardon I have been out only half an hour. He who neither knows how to be a father, a husband, a son, nor a friend, is not an honest man.

264.

pretendere, *to pretend*

sciocchezza { *nonsense* / *stupidity*

pagina, *page*

val più, *is more worth*.

Non ho mai veduto un tal imbecille come voi, che sciocchezza avete fatto, vi aveva detto di comperarmi mezza dozzina di penne d'acciajo e voi non me ne portato che una — Guardate che bella ragazza, se fossi pittore vorrei fare il suo ritratto. Le avete mai parlato? No perchè io sono inglese ed essa è tedesca e non potremmo capirci l'un l'altro. Che peccato! Mi dicono che è una ragazza d'ingegno. Conoscete sua madre? Sì essa è vedova, ed è una delle più abili modiste della nostra città. — Povero me, che noioso libro mi avete prestato, non ho letto che la prima pagina e ne sono già stanco. Un uomo d'ingegno povero val più che dieci imbecilli ricchi.— Povero me, come me la caverò? Parlatene a vostro zio egli è avvocato e potrà darvi un buon consiglio. — Se dite un' altra volta una tale sciocchezza, sarete punito. Siate amico dei buoni e nemico dei cattivi. — Avete molti amici ? Ho un amico ma molte conoscenze; chi pretende di aver più di un amico non ne ha nessuno. Se un amico è infelice bisogna aiutarlo, se un nemico non bisogna rallegrarsene.

265.

Si elide l'articolo:

1° Innanzi ai sostantivi presi in un senso generale p. e.:

History is an excellent teacher, La storia è ottima maestra, dirò invece: *The history of England is agreeable*, perchè qui non parlo più della storia in generale ma di una data storia speciale.

2° Innanzi ai nomi propri di persona e geografici e ai titoli che li procedono p. e.:

king Alfred, il re Alfredo.

Sono eccettuati i titoli con desinenza femminile, come *princess* o qualche titolo maschile come *Emperor*. Tra i nomi geografici sono eccettuati mari o fiumi.

3° Innanzi alle parole:

hell, inferno	*paradise*, paradiso
earth, terra	*heaven*, cielo.
pride, orgoglio	*Irish*, irlandese
to fall into, sboccare	*degree*, grado
as though, come se	*foreign*, straniero
to ascend, salire	*on board*, a bordo
worthy, degno di	*fate*, destino
adversity, avversità	*to mix*, mischiarsi

to be badly paired, star male assieme.

Men are born with two eyes and one tongue as though they should see twice as much as they say. Adversity is an excellent teacher. Doctor Johnson was asked whether he liked music. No, said he, but of all noises, I think music is the least disagreeable. Queen Victoria is said to be very fond of the italian music. Pride and poverty are badly paired. The pride and poverty of the Irish are both in a high degree. Do you like history? Yes. Have you studied the history of England? Yes thoroughly. Who drove the Danes out of England? King Alfred the great. Do you like horses? Yes the horse (*) is a noble animal. I prefer dogs, the dog is faithful. The Emperor Peter the Great has travelled very much, he amused himself in mixing with the people as though he were one of them. The princess Mary is very fond of foreign

---

(*) Il nome al singolare dell'individuo coll'articolo serve per indicare tutta la specie.

tongues, she speaks english perfectly well. Did you never ascend mount St. Bernard? Yes once. By whom was the cape of Good Hope discovered? By Vasco di Gama, a Spaniard. The Severn is the largest river in England. The Danube falls into the black sea. Bonaparte went on board the Belerophon, but sailed on board the Nothumberland to St. Helena, he was, perhaps, worthy a better fate.

266.

ignoranza, *ignorance*   presunzione, *presumption*
umanità, *mankind* (*)   civiltà, *civility*
suddito, *subject*   elefante, *elephant*.

Egli mi pregò di andare a chiamare il dottor Antonio, e perchè non l'ho trovato egli mi sgridò, come se io fossi obbligato di andarlo a cercare per tutta la città. L'ignoranza e la presunzione stanno male assieme. L'ignoranza della principessa Maria e l'orgoglio del re Francesco sono ben conosciuti nel paese. Si dice che l'elefante sia l'animale più intelligente dopo l'uomo. I cavalli e i buoi furono utilissimi all'umanità, senza di essi la civiltà non sarebbe stata possibile. Il Volga è il più gran fiume d'Europa, esso sbocca nel mar Caspio. Dicevano al re Alessandro il Grande che egli era simile agli dei, ma quando egli prese un raffreddore per essersi gettato nel fiume egli comprese che non era che un mortale come i suoi sudditi. Salendo sul monte S. Bernardo si gode una magnifica vista. (**)

267.

Non si mette il partitivo (*some any* innanzi al sostantivi, quando non sulla quantità ma sulla qualità dell'oggetto si vuol chiamar l'attenzione così:

He sells paper pens and ink, Egli vende carta penne e inchiostro, mentre si dirà *He has sold some paper and books*,

(*) Nel senso di genere umano; sebbene parola impropria, perchè di uso generale crediamo esserne scusati.
(**) *magnificent view*.

perchè nel primo caso io annunzio la qualità degli oggetti che uno vende, nel secondo caso annunzio che ha venduto una certa quantità di quei tali oggetti che già si sapeva tener egli'in vendita.

Le parole *as, too, how, however, so,* vogliono prima l'aggettivo poi l'articolo e infine il sostantivo p. e :

I have seldom read so beautiful a book.

Si mette l'articolo *a* innanzi a un nome o aggettivo che accompagna il nome al singolare rinchiuso in una frase incidente p. e.:

Joseph, a skilful painter, set out for Paris, Giuseppe, abile pittore, partì per Parigi.

lecture, rimprovero	*trespass,* mancanza
venial, veniale	*besides,* inoltre
xi	*to utter,* proferire
fright, spavento	*orange,* melarancia
to help to, offrire	*wares,* merci.

Why have you scolded that boy? Because he refused to answer to my question. You are too severe a teacher, you have given him too sharp a lecture for so venial a trespass, besides he vas in such a fright that he could not utter a word. There was no reason for his fright, I assure you he deserved the sharp lecture I have given him. The water of the Parmessus, a small river in Beotia, inspired the poets of Antiquity. Upon what does that man live? Upon his industry. What does he sell? He sells cloth, linen, and shirts. Has he sold any shirts to day? He has sold some cloth but not any shirts, and therefore he is deficient in money. May I help you to some (*) coffee? I thank you, I never take any. Mr. Massa, a clever merchant, sells clothes at a very moderate price. Italy produces oranges limons and oil. Go and buy me some oranges, I am thirsty. May I help you to some cigars? I thank you, I do not smoke.

(*) Quando si offre qualchecosa, comunque la frase sia interrogativa si adopera *some* invece di *any* perchè per civiltà si deve supporre che uno accetti ciò che gli si offre.

268.

contemporaneo, *contemporary*   coloniale, *colonial*
torturare, *to torture*   carbone, *coal*.

Perchè avete fatto così aspro rimprovero a mio fratello? Perchè non proferì una parola quando gli ordinava di parlare, inoltre voi sapete, io non posso sopportare un ragazzo così fiero. Egli dice che voi siete un maestro troppo severo, e che non può proferir parola senza che lo sgridiate. (*) Galileo uomo superiore ai suoi contemporanei, fu torturato dai nemici della verità. Il padre del nostro amico Carlo, uomo d'ingegno e prode ufficiale, fu ferito alla battaglia di Custoza il 24 Giugno 1866, ora non è più ufficiale, egli è mercante di caffè, zucchero e altre merci coloniali. Le merci che mi avete spedito non sono buone a nulla, dovrò rimandarvele, perchè merci così cattive non possono esser vendute in un paese così ricco. Posso offrirvi del tè? Obbligatissimo, amo molto il tè. Prendete zucchero. Vi ringrazio, non metto mai zucchero nel tè. Avrei comperato fazzoletti di tela, ma siccome egli non conosce l'inglese, non sapeva come fare per capirlo, e dovetti andare da un altro mercante, che vende le sue merci a un prezzo molto moderato. L'Inghilterra produce carbone e ferro. Avete mandato il domestico a comperar carbone per la stufa? L'ho mandato ma non è ancora ritornato.

269.

to strike, { battere / abbattere / colpire }   *struck, struck.*
   colonnello, *colnel* (**)
avventura, *adventure*   granaio, *granary*
improvvisamente, *abruptly*   uva, *grape*
mi fece servire, *he had served me*   dopo di che, *whereupon*.

(*) *without your scolding him.*
(**) pronuncisi *coernel*.

Quando l'orologio batte le dieci venite a chiamarmi, sono stato invitato dal dottor Guglielmo e mi rincrescerebbe moltissimo se arrivassi troppo tardi. Mi fece servire con una tale gentilezza che non potei a meno di ringraziarlo caldamente prima d'andarmene. Vi era pure il colonello Maurizio, giovane spiritoso che ci raccontò le sue avventure. Quando batterono le undici il dottor Guglielmo ci fece servire dell'eccellente Sciampagna; il colonnello Maurizio ne bevette dieci bicchieri dopo di che si alzò improvvisamente e senza proferir parola se ne andò. Noi fummo colpiti di meraviglia e tutti dicevano che non era una condotta degna di un signore cosi gentile. Quando lo vidi gli dissi: Mio caro signore, voi ve ne andaste troppo improvvisamente, che fu? Mio caro, mi rispose, temeva di ubriacarmi. — Perchè avete abbattuto quel magnifico albero che avevate nel vostro giardino? Perchè non produceva più frutti. Che cosa produce la vostra campagna? Grano ed uva. L'ho battuto perchè ha mangiato uva del mio giardino. Povero me, mi hanno rubato tutto il grano e l'uva che c'era nel granaio. Egli fu colpito da spavento ma non proferì parola.

270.

towards (toords), verso
shallow, da poco, futile
meanly, meschinamente
XIX
jealous, geloso

the egg, l'uovo
courtier, cortigiano
entreprise, impresa
foreigner, forestiere
to assign, assegnare.

THE EGG OF COLUMBUS.

Pedro Gonzales de Mendoza the Grand Cardinal of Spain, invited Columbus to a banquet, where he assigned him the most honourable place at table, and had him served with the ceremonies which, in those punctilious times, were observed towards sovereigns. At this repast is said to have occurred the well known anecdote of the egg. A shallow courtier present, impatient of the honors paid to Columbus, and meanly jealous of him as a foreigner, abruptly asked him whether he thought that in case he had not discovered the Indies, there were not other men who would be capable of the enterprise. To this Columbus made no immediate reply, but taking an egg, invited the company to make it stand upon one end. Every one attempted it, but in vain, whereupon he struck it upon the table so as to break the end, and left it standing on the broken part; illustrating in this simple manner, that when he had once shown the way to the new world, nothing was easier than to follow it. Oh! cried then out many gentlemen of the company, in that manner it is not difficult. No, it is not, replied Columbus, but why did you not do it before me?

Conversation.

Question.	Answers.
Who invited Columbus to a banquet?	*Pedro Gonzales de Mendoza, the Grand Cardinal of Spain.*
What place did he assign him at table?	*He assigned him the most honorable place at table.*
How did he serve him?	*He served him with the ceremonies which were observed towards sovereigns.*
What is said to have occurred at this repast?	*The well known anecdote of the egg is said to have occurred at this repast.*
Of what was a shallow courtier impatient?	*He was impatient of the honors paid to Columbus.*
Why was he jealous of him?	*Because he was a foreigner.*

What did he ask him?	He asked him abruptly, whether he thought that in case he had not discovered the Indies, there were no other men who would be capable of the enterprise.
Did Columbus answer?	No, he made no immediate reply.
What did he do then?	He took an egg, and invited the company to make it stand upon one end.
Did they attempt it?	Yes, they did, but in vain.
How did then Columbus manage it?	He struck the egg upon the table so as to break the end, and left it standing on the broken part.
What would he illustrate by that?	That when he had once shown the way to the new world, nothing was easier than to follow it.
What did many gentlemen of the company cry out?	They cried out: Oh! in that manner, it is not difficult.
What was Columbus'reply?	No, it is not, answered he, but why did you not do it before me?

Ripetizione.

Ditemi in inglese l'infinito passato e participio passato di *colpire, battere*. — Da che cosa devono esser preceduti i nomi di nazionalità, professione ecc.? In quali casi si elide l'articolo? In quale invece lo si mette a differenza dell'italiano? Qual'è la costruzione della frase quando ci sono le parole *such, what, how, however, so* ecc.? Quand'è che non si fa uso dei partitivi *some, any?* Quando adoprasi *some* nell'interrogare?

Lezione trentesima sesta. Lesson the thirty sixth.

SINTASSI E PARTICOLARITÀ DEL SOSTANTIVO.

271.

Generalmente, se la frase non è interrogativa il soggetto (sostantivo o pronome) si mette prima del verbo, però nelle narrazioni, dopo i verbi mediante i quali si riferiscono parole altrui, come: *to say, to exclaim, to reply*, il soggetto si mette dopo, p e.:

You shall be hanged immediately, exclaimed the king.

Nelle interrogazioni negative, il soggetto se è sostantivo si mette dopo *not*, se è pronome prima, p. e.:

Is not France a delightful country?
Is he not an idle fellow?

Quando più nomi sono uniti mediante le congiunzioni disgiuntive *either, or, neither, nor* allora il verbo s'accorda coll'ultimo nome, p. e.:

Either your brother or his has done it.

I nomi collettivi vogliono il verbo al singolare o al plurale secondo l'intenzione di voler far risaltare l'unità del corpo, o la pluralità dei membri.

to jest, scherzare
the police, la polizia
chief, principale
to doom, destinare

to dissolve, sciogliere
eagerly, ardentemente
this day week, oggi a otto
contest, lotta

Is not my brother invited? Neither he nor you nor any one of the family is invited. — I wonder whether it is you or your friend who has written this. Neither

I nor my brother knows the german language, therefore it is quite impossible we have written it. — Did you hear the news? I heard nothing, what is the matter? The parliament was dissolved. You are jesting, I don't believe you. Yet it is a fact. And do you know, why it was dissolved? I am told they were divided in opinion, and the minister could not help dissolving it. At this sad news, the crowd was immense before the house, but they were all dispersed by the police. The multitude eagerly pursue pleasure as their chief good. Do you know when is parliament to meet? I think this day week. My family is my only happiness in the world, I have always all them around me. Either Cesar or Pompey was doomed to fall in the contest.

272.

fiducia, *confidence*
curare, *to cure*

chiacchierare, *to chatt*
d'altro, *of something else*.

Perchè corre la folla tanto? Si dice che il re o il principe si presenterà alla finestra per salutare il popolo e ringraziarlo della fiducia che ha avuto in essi durante la passata guerra. Dicono che il parlamento si debba riunire oggi a otto ma non lo credo perchè il ministero non è ancora formato, e nè il re nè il principe non sono arrivati. — Se aveste più fiducia nel vostro medico egli vi curerebbe con più amore. — Non ha il popolo fiducia nel parlamento? No, perchè chiacchiera troppo. Ha ragione. — Quando entrai nella stanza, il padrone sgridava il servo, siete un briccone, gli disse egli con collera. Voi siete un briccone, disse il servo, io sono un uomo onesto. — Perchè fu dispersa la folla dalla polizia? Non so se la principessa o la regina fu insultata. Non fu disciolto il parlamento? Non ancora ma oggi a otto il ministero lo scioglierà. — Non è arrivato il procuratore? Arriverà oggi a otto. — Se credete che il bene principale sia il denaro v'ingannate. — Parliamo d'altro non mi piace scherzare su ciò. Napoleone III fu destinato a cadere nella lotta contro i tedeschi.

273.

an ugly book, un libraccio *a fine little book*, un libriccino
a little table, un tavolino *a large book*, un librone.

Non essendovi in inglese (*) alcuna forma che corrisponda ai diminutivi e aumentativi, vezzeggiativi, o spregiativi italiani, bisogna renderli in inglese traducendo il senso della desinenza col mezzo degli aggettivi che fanno al caso.

I sostantivi inglesi possono quasi tutti diventare aggettivi mediante l'aggiunta della terminazione del part. pass. *ed*.

hair, capelli *haired* con capelli
A *yellow haired girl*, una ragazza da'capelli biondi.
A *long bearded hero*, un eroe dalla lunga barba
A *black eyed woman*, una donna dagli occhi neri
light headed, di testa leggera, sventato
fair, bello *middle aged*, di mezza età
if you choose, se desiderate *little sized*, di piccola statura
to fall in love, innamorarsi *to court*, corteggiare.

Do you like that yellow haired girl who is playing at cards with that long bearded young man? I don't think, she is very pretty she has an ugly large foot; I prefer that black eyed woman who is chatting on the side of the middle aged and little sized gentleman; she has a very pretty little hand and she is very witty. — That light headed young man has forgotten to put the address in a lettre he has sent to his parents the 30th last. I should very like to be acquainted with that fair black

---

(*) meno pochissime eccezioni.

haired girl, I am quite fallen in love with her. Are you?
Do you know her parents? Yes, that middle aged gentleman who wears spectacles is her father, and that little sized black dressed lady is her mother. And what are they? The father is a counselor and the mother was a milliner. If you choose I will introduce you to them, that you may court the little fair girl, with whom you are in love. You are the best natured fellow I ever knew, you will exceedingly oblige me: and when will you introduce me to them? If you choose, come and see me on Saturday evening, we shall go to the ambassador's ball, where I am told they are to go.

274.

Se non foste un giovane così sventato potreste aspirare alla mano di quella bella ragazzina dai capelli biondi di cui mi avete detto che siete innamorato, ma che non osate corteggiare per timore di essere deriso. Sarei l'uomo più felice della terra se potessi baciare quella gentil manina, ma temo ch'essa ne ami un altro. E chi credete voi che essa ami? Quel signore di piccola statura dai capelli neri che la corteggiava l'altra sera dall'ambasciatore inglese. Non credo ch'essa sia di così cattivo gusto. Guardate quella signora dai grandi occhi neri che balla con quel signore dalla lunga barba, che bel piedino essa ha. Voi non pensate ad altro che ai bei piedini delle belle signore, fareste meglio a pensare ai vostri debiti. Vi chieggo scusa, ho abbastanza occasione di pensare ai miei debiti quando i miei creditori dal cuor duro vengono a trovarmi. Povero me, che libracci leggete! Non potete che guastarvi lo spirito leggendo di tali libri. Eccovi un libriccino che leggerete sicuramente con piacere.

275.

Quando i sostantivi che indicano rapporti personali, come parentela, amicizia, impieghi ecc., non sono accompagnati dall'art. definito, essi vogliono la preposizione *to* innanzi al loro complemento:

He is secretary to the minister. She is mother to the poor.

Il soggetto plurale vuole allo stesso numero i sostantivi e i pronomi che vi si riferiscono; così:

Many people lost their lives, moltissimi vi perdettero la vita.

a meno che l'oggetto posseduto non sia una cosa comune a tutti i membri rappresentati dal sostantivo plurale; così:

These children lost their father.

to throw, gettare   *threw*   *thrown*   *stone*, pietra
to get rid of, sbarazzarsi di   *prisoner*, prigioniero
of course { naturalmente   *estate*, bene, terra
           certamente   *shamefully*, vergognosamente

Are you not ashamed to speak with that gentleman? Why then? Don't you know he was secretary to the prince, who was obliged to get rid of him because he had deceived him most shamefully. I didn't know that, he has always been a friend to me, and his wife is really a mother te the poor and to the unfortunate. You must ged rid of him, he is not worthy of your friendship. Of course I'll, but I am sorry.—Who has thrown that book on the earth? That light headed young man threw it because he was tired with reading. I wonder how your uncle became so rich! Don't you know he was heir to all the prince's estates? Is he a friend to the poor? Of course he is because he is a good hearted fellow. Gentlemen to your healths. To yours. Who is at present the president of the parliament? Mr. Cairoli, all his brothers lost their lives for their country. Heroic family they are, are they not? Of course and admired and loved by every body. Why don't you get rid of that idle fellow? He is a good companion to my children and I cannot get rid of him. Why did you throw that poor cat out of the window? I threw it out, because otherwise I could not get rid of it.

276.

Quando era segretario del ministro, mi divertivo moltissimo, andava spesso a caccia con lui, e mi invitava quasi ogni giorno a pranzo. Quando egli morì, sua moglie, crede di tutti i suoi beni, si sbarazzò di me come di un vecchio servo. Giovanni perchè avete gettato via quel cucchiajo? Lo gettai via perchè era troppo sporco. Signori, mi prendo la libertà di bere alla vostra salute. Vorreste esser l'erede dei miei beni? Certamente. Allora sbarazzatevi dei cattivi amici dai quali siete ingannato. Lo farò certamente poichè lo desiderate. Miei figli, amate la vita poichè essa è un bene (*) ma se la patria ne ha bisogno, datela volentieri per essa, guardate quanto sono ammirati coloro che hanno perduto la vita per questa madre amatissima. Quando i prigionieri passarono, la folla gettò loro pietre sulla testa tanto erano disprezzati.

277.

I nomi di nazionalità sebbene che indicando la qualità dovrebbero essere considerati quali aggettivi e però essere invariabili, tuttavia ricevono generalmente la *s* al plurale, meno quelli che finiscono per *sh ch*. In questi casi per distinguere il sesso si usa aggiungere *man* e *woman* e allora formerebbero il plurale regolarmente

an *Englishman*   an *Englishwoman*
two *English*, two *Englishmen*   two *English*, two *Englishwomen*

I nomi di cose e di animali di cui non importa indicare il sesso sono, come sappiamo, neutri; a questa regola fanno eccezione:

(*) *good*.

1° *ship*, vascello che è femminile come pure tutti i nomi di vascelli;
2° *moon*, luna pure femminile e 3° *sun*, sole che è maschile. I nomi di paesi adoperati in senso personale sono femminili

to distinguish one'self, distinguersi   *throne*, trono
inconsiderateness, sconsideratezza   *superfluous*, superfluo
acknowledged, riconosciuto   *make haste*, fate presto
perseverance, perseveranza.   *cloud*, nube
dutch, olandese.

The English distinguish themselves by their industry, the Scotch by their perseverance, and the Irish by their inconsiderateness. — And by what do the French and Dutch distinguish themselves? The French love glory, and the Dutch first of all, money, and then God. — Yesterday I met two Englishmen, and four Englishwomen, three Frenchmen, and five Frenchwomen, some Scotchmen, and Scotchwomen, Irishmen and Irishwomen, and several other amiable ladies and gentlemen at Almack's. — Who is that woman there? She is an Englishwoman. — Who is the lady with whom you have just spoken? She is a young Frenchwoman. — At the meeting of the naturalists in London, besides Englishmen and Frenchmen, there were Germans, Romans, Bavarians, Belgians, Prussians, Italians, and other nations present. — Brittannia sits on her invincible throne, the acknowledged queen of the ocean; she extends her strong but mild dominion over two hundred milions of men. — France sends her superfluous sons to fight against the children of the deserts of Africa. — The sun will not shine to day, he is covered by the clouds. What did you do yesterday evening in Regent's Park? I was looking at the moon as she was rising. The ship Prince Charles is arrived last week, make haste if you wish to see her, I am told she'll set out on thursday.

278.

mi pare. *methinks*   mi pareva, *methought*.

La sconsideratezza degl'Irlandesi è proverbiale; una volta due tedeschi chiesero ad una irlandese se capiva il tedesco; certamente, rispose essa, purché lo si parli in irlandese. Un altra volta due italiani raccontavano ad una francese che era morto un uomo di cento e dieci anni e la francese se ne meravigliava; non v'è nulla di straordinario, esclamò un irlandese che era in loro compagnia, se mio nonno vivesse, avrebbe ora centotrent'anni. Mi pare che voi sherziate. No davvero. — La Prussia è una grande nazione, essa ha l'armata più forte in Europa, i suoi generali sono i più istruiti. L'Italia è riconosciuta per essere un bellissimo paese, se i suoi abitanti fossero meno pigri essa sarebbe la prima nazione d'Europa. Mi pareva di udire che quei signori fossero tedeschi. Vi siete ingannato sono spagnuoli. Mi pare che voi conosciate molto bene la lingua spagnuola. Mi pareva di udire un rumore, ma mi sono ingannato. Fate presto altrimenti non arriverete in tempo. Mi pareva che il vascello partisse alle cinque. No esso parte alle quattro. Come si chiama? Luigi XIV.

279.

ricerca, *researche*
imbrogliare ⎫
confondere ⎬ *to puzzle*
malgrado ⎱ *notwithstanding*
         ⎰ *in spite of*

riescire a, *to succed in*
essere confuso, *to be puzzled*
tiro ⎫
burla ⎬ *trick*
astuzia ⎭

Egli non riescirà mai a trovare buoni amici, perché è un giovane sventato e fa sempre dei brutti tiri ai suoi compagni. Certamente, avete ragione, però egli è giovane di buon cuore e merita di essere amato malgrado le burle ch'egli fa ai suoi amici. Malgrado le sue ricerche non riuscì a trovare la ragazza dagli occhi neri della quale era innamorato. Egli se ne andò tutto confuso perchè malgrado le sue astuzie non era riescito ad imbrogliarmi. Non riuscì la folla ad entrare nel palazzo? No perchè i soldati la dispersero. Non era egli confuso quando sono entrato? Non lo credo, perchè pensate che fosse confuso? Perchè sapeva che era in collera con lui per il brutto tiro che mi aveva fatto.

280.

to undergo, subire
his own, suo proprio
suddenly, improvvisamente
neither, nessuno dei due
lest, per timore che
to evince, provare
the roguery, la furfanteria
to rouse, destare
to restore, restituire

burst out into a laughter, diede in uno scroscio di risa.

THE SAGACIOUS INDIAN.

A Peruvian, who had been robbed of a horse, made diligent researches to find out the thief, at last he succeeded in discovering it was a Spaniard. He gave notice of the fact to the magistrate of the place, and the parties were ordered to appear. The Spaniard swore the horse was his own, and that he had him since many years. The poor Indian, having no proofs to produce, would have lost his cause; but suddenly he threw his cloak over the horse's head and turning towards the Spaniard: You assure, said he, you possess this horse since many years, then you will of course be able of telling us of which eye he is blind. The Spaniard was quite puzzled at so unexpected a question, however, lest he should rouse suspicion by his hesitation, he answered: he is blind of the left. The Indian burst out into a laughter: methinks, said he, throwing off the cloak, you know indeed your horse very well, he is blind of neither. The judge now perceived the roguery of the Spaniard, sent him into prison to undergo afterwards the punishment he deserved, and having restored the horse to the Peruvian, expressed him his admiration of the trick he had made use of to evince his rights.

Conversation.

Question.	Answers.
Of what had a Peruvian been robbed of?	*He had been robbed of a horse.*
Did he try to find out the thief?	*Yes, he made diligent researches to this purpose.*
Were they of any success?	*Yes, for he succeeded in discovering it was a Spaniard.*
What did he do then?	*He gave notice of the fact to the magistrate of the place.*
What was the consequence of it?	*The parties were ordered to appear.*
Did the Spaniard confess his theft?	*No, he did not, but swore, on the contrary, that he had the horse since many years.*
What would nearly have been the consequence of the denial?	*The Indian would nearly have lost his cause.*
Why so?	*Because he had no proofs to produce.*
How did he act then?	*He suddenly threw his cloak over the horse's head.*

Towards whom did he turn?	He turned towards the Spaniard.
What question did he put him?	You assure, said he, you possess this horse since many years, you will then of course be able of telling us of which eye he is blind.
Did the Spaniard immediately give an answer?	No, for he was at first puzzled by that unexpected question.
And was he long so?	No, he gave soon an answer.
Why then?	Lest his hesitation should rouse suspicion.
What did he answer?	That the horse was blind of the left eye.

Ripetizione.

Qual è il posto del soggetto, quando si riferiscono le parole altrui? Quale nelle frasi interrogative-negative? Come si accorda il verbo quando più nomi sono uniti da *either, or, neither, nor*? Come si accordano i nomi collettivi? Come si formano i diminutivi aumentativi, vezzeggiativi? Che cosa si aggiunge al sostantivo per formarne un aggettivo? Da qual preposizione sono seguiti i nomi che esprimono relazioni personali? Di che genere sono i nomi di paesi in senso personale? e di vascelli? Come fanno il plurale i nomi di nazionalità che finiscono per *sh, ch*? Ditemi l'infinito passato e participio passato del verbo *gettare*.

Lezione trentesima settima. Lesson the thirty seventh.

SINTASSI E PARTICOLARITÀ DEGLI AGGETTIVI.

281.

L'aggettivo qualificativo che per regola abbiamo visto precedere il sostantivo, lo segue invece nei seguenti casi:

1° Quando l'aggettivo ha un complemento da cui non può esser disgiunto, p. e.

He is a man capable of any thing, È uomo capace di qualunque cosa.

2° Quando serve di soprannome p. e.

Pepin the short, Peppino il breve.

3° Gli aggettivi di dimensione che si mettono dopo il nome esprimente la misura.

4° Gli aggettivi formati da altre parti del discorso mediante l'aggiunta dell' *a*, p. e.

asleep addormentato, *alive* vivo, *ajar* socchiuso, *alike* simile.

Dopo il comparativo si elide in inglese la negazione p. e.

È più ricco che non si crede, *He is richer than is thought*.

devoted, dedito
by how much? di quanto?
by. an inch, di un pollice
pitiless, senza pietà
hard, duro, crudele

commerce, commercio
science, scienza
pot, vaso
stranger, straniero
by far, di gran lunga.

Tarquin the Proud was driven from Rome in the year 534. — The English are a people much devoted to commerce, but also to sciences. — A man devoted to game is a lost man. — Look at those men asleep, why are they in such a state? The waiter has brought a pot full of beer and they have drunk the whole of it. — Bring a pot full of water, if you please, we are all very thirsty. He was a man kind to his friends and civil to strangers. Is not that cloak as large as mine? No, it is by an inch smaller. By how much is your brother taller than I? By three inches. And your uncle? He is by two inches shorter than you. How strong is a company? A company is a hundred and fifty man strong, and a batallion is five hundred man strong. Is not Paris as large as London? No it is not half so large. — It is not certainly we who are hard to the poor, nor you neither, are you? for, who could be pitiless to the miserable? — I am at a loss how to find two hundred francs, which I want for to morrow; your friend Charles owes me more than four hundred, but he seems not to be disposed to pay them to me. Write to his father. Do you think he will pay his son's debts? Yes, he is by far richer than is thought. — That poor boy is too lightly clothed, I dare say, he will catch a cold. Never fear, he is stronger than is believed.

282.

ubriaco, *drunk*   ubriachezza, *drunkness*
educare, *to educate*   patria, *fatherland*.

    La vostra casa non è essa alta quanto la mia? Non lo credo, la mia è alta 80 piedi. Ho veduto un uomo addormentato nel vostro giardino, che ha egli? Egli è ubbriaco, egli ha bevuto il vaso pieno di vino. È un peccato che sia dedito all'ubriachezza, è un uomo amato da tutti quelli che lo conoscono, perchè gentile con tutti, ed anche persona molto abile negli affari e che potrebbe fare la felicità dei suoi. (*) Napoleone il Grande fu ammirato da tutto il mondo. Perchè siete voi senza pietà con quella povera famiglia? Ho per essa più pietà che non pare. Ma essa non merita la pietà degli uomini onesti; il padre è un uomo pigro dedito solo al giuoco, egli educò si male i suoi figli che ora sono persone buone a nulla e dedite all'ubriachezza. Non è Firenze bella quanto Napoli? No, Napoli é di gran lunga più bella. Quanto vale questo panno nero? Esso vale quattro franchi il braccio, ma guardate esso è alto due braccia e un quarto. Io abbisogno panno alto tre braccia. Se aveste educato meglio i vostri figli sarebbero ora utili a sè ed alla patria. Li ho educati con maggior cura che non crediate, ma tutto fu sgraziatamente inutile.

283.

the dancing master, il maestro di ballo
singing lessons, lezioni di canto.

Il participio presente posto innanzi ai nomi serve spesso da aggettivo. Alle volte il participio presente unito ad un aggettivo forma un aggettivo composto, di cui la prima parte soltanto si modifica nel comparativo e superlativo; così:

fine looking, di bell' aspetto
finer looking, di più bell' aspetto
riding lessons, lezioni di cavalcare

to waste away, sprecare
it may be, può darsi
delighting, delizioso
enchanting, incantevole
blooming, fiorente

first rate, di prima classe
to fence, tirar di scherma
to have objection, aver in contrario
obliging, obligante, cortese.

I am told your dancing master has fallen in love with that fine looking girl whose father is physician to the king. It may be, she is very pretty and besides she is

(*) *of his family.*

a first rate singing teacher. Do you permit me, father, to take some singing lessons from her? I have not the least objection, provided you do not waste your time and money away by chatting with her. Has she a delighting voice? O yes, a very delighting one. Where do you live at present? On the Poggio Imperiale, we enjoy there an enchanting view. What has become of that bad-looking man's son? He has become a first rate dancing master, he gains more than five hundred francs a month, and has married the finest looking girl I ever saw. Do not waste your time away when you are young, otherwise you will repent when old. I never knew such an obliging man as your fencing master.

284.

Mi dicono che ho una voce deliziosa, se non aveste nulla in contrario, vorrei prendere alcune lezioni di canto, conosco appunto un maestro di canto di prima classe, che mi fu presentato jer l'altro dalla mia amica Carlotta, se non avete nulla in contrario lo manderò a chiamare e comincerò subito. Non ho nulla in contrario, se avete una voce deliziosa prendete lezione di canto ma badate di non sprecare il denaro. Che cosa è divenuto di quel florente ragazzo di bello aspetto che giuocava spesso col mio a Boboli? Di chi è egli figlio? Egli è mio figlio, signore. Davvero? Me ne congratulo. Siete troppo buono signore voi lo adulate, il vostro ha un aspetto di gran lunga migliore del mio. E che cosa n'è di lui? Egli prende lezioni di scherma. Ha egli un buon maestro di scherma? Certamente, di prima classe. Il mio preferisce prender lezioni di cavalcare; egli è molto amante del cavalcare e ha avuto la fortuna di trovare un maestro di cavalcare di prima classe e nello stesso tempo un uomo molto cortese cogli scolari.

Le parti del corpo che abbiamo visto ricevere l'aggettivo possessivo, vogliono l'articolo definito quando nella frase fanno l'ufficio di complemento indiretto, ossia che sono preceduti da una preposizione.

take me by the hand, prendetemi per la mano.

Own, proprio, si aggiunge agli aggettivi per dar maggior forza.

young ones i bambini
little ones e i piccoli delle bestie.

Invece di *much* e *many* si può usare

a great deal, a great many, plenty of.

altro { *other*, che non è quello di prima
      { *else*, aggiuntivo-si mette dopo il nome.

to hide, nascondere	*hid* *hidden*.
ear, orecchio	*to bring up*, allevare
show to, condurre	*carefully*, accuratamente
monkey, scimmia	*to act*, agire.

Why are you angry with your son? He has been very wild at school, the master took him by the ear and drove him out shamefully. You must take care of your little ones and bring them up very carefully if you wish they do not become wild. The monkey is very tender of its little ones. Is it? Yes, It hides them carefully when the enemy approaches. Why have you hidden so carefully your umbrella? I hid it because I was afraid somebody could steal it. A woman must have a great deal of patience with her little ones. Of course she must. English people are something proud because they have plenty of money. Have you any thing else to tell me? Nothing, sir. — Give me the other, this one is good for nothing. — He promised to rise early this morning, but one thing is to speak another to act. Do you want any thing else? I want a great many things, but you cannot give me any thing. When the blind man approaches take him by the hand and show him to his seat. Where is the monkey which your father brought from America? It has hidden itself. You mistake, it is in the garden I have seen it with my own eyes. I pity that poor fellow, his children have been brought up without any care, and now they are good for nothing.

286.

Sapreste dirmi dove s'è nascosta la scimmia? Non lo so davvero, la sarà forse nel giardino in cerca dei suoi piccoli dei quali essa è molto tenera. Ho veduto una gran quantità di scimmie in America. Ogni animale è tenero dei suoi piccoli. È una cosa del tutto naturale, pure vi sono donne che dimenticano i bambini per i divertimenti. — Che cosa avete nella testa, che scorre il sangue? Qualcuno m'ha gettato una pietra sulla testa e poi s'è nascosto. Perchè si nasconde vostra nipote? La si vergogna perchè fu cacciata vergognosamente dalla scuola. C'erano tanti sbagli nei temi di vostro figlio, che voleva prenderlo per l'orecchio e cacciarlo fuori vergognosamente, ma egli si nascose così accuratamente che non potei trovarlo. Voi siete senza pietà coi poveri, ma avete torto perchè sebbene avete molti denari, potete anche voi aver bisogno degli altri. Nascondete accuratamente i vostri libri altrimenti i vostri bambini potrebbero sciuparli. Come vendete questa tela? Due franchi il braccio(*).Quanto è alta? Un braccio e mezzo. Non ne avete dell'altra alta un braccio? Eccone. Questa non mi piace, l'altra è più fina. Avete bisogno altro? Per ora, no. Quando arrivate a Roma dite a quell'imbecille di Giovanni che sono molto in collera con lui perchè non progredisce nei suoi studi

(*) ell.

e che lo consiglio di prendere anche lezioni di scherma per diventare più forte. Non mancherò, devo dirgli qualcosa altro? Niente altro, addio.

287.

per timore che, *lest* — abbondante, *plentiful*
le mura *the walls* — lo stato maggiore, *the staff*
rinfresco, *refreshment* — star in guardia, *to be on one's guard*
di cuore, *heartily* — metter in ordine, *to settle*.

Vi ringrazio di cuore per il vostro gentile invito, subito che avrò messo in ordine i miei affari non mancherò di approfittarne. Avete a fare con un briccone, state in guardia per timore che egli non v'inganni. Perchè nascondete così accuratamente il vostro denaro? Quando si viaggia e si ha da fare con ogni sorta di persone bisogna star in guardia per timore di esser derubati. Egli corse a casa spaventato e giurò di aver veduto coi suoi propri occhi lo stato maggiore nemico a poca distanza dalle mura della città. Bisogna, disse allora suo padre, nascondere accuratamente tutto il danaro, per timore che i soldati irrompano nella città e ci rubino ogni cosa. Ho avuto la fortuna di fare jeri la conoscenza del sig. Vanni, ufficiale dello stato maggiore. Io ho fatto la sua conoscenza due anni fa da mio zio il generale, egli è una persona molto cortese con tutti e tenero della sua famiglia, mi si dice che tutti i giorni egli prende per la mano i suoi bambini, e li conduce a fare una passeggiata sopra le mura della città dove si gode un'aria rinfrescante e una vista incantevole. Volete qualche rinfresco? Vi ringrazio di cuore per la vostra gentile offerta, ma non ho bisogno di nulla, sono stato da mio cugino l'ofliciale di stato maggiore, il quale mi fece servire una abbondante colazione e mi è del tutto impossibile di prendere qualcosa altro.

288.

the monk, il monaco	to entertain, trattare, convitare
afterwards, dopo	to deceive, ingannare
guest, ospite	to lull, quetare, addormentare
meal, pasto	to pledge, far brindisi
deadly, mortale	poison, veleno

DESPERATE PATRIOTISM.

During the wars of Napoleon in Spain, a regiment of the guard of Jerome, ex-king of Westphalia, arived under the walls of Figueiras.

The general sent a message to the prior to demand, if he would prepare any refreshments for his officers and men. The prior replied, that the men would find good quarters in the town, but that he and his monks would entertain the general and his staff.

About an hour afterwards, a plentiful dinner was served, but the general knowing by experience, how necessary it was for the French to be on their guard, when eating and drinking with Spaniards, lest they be deceived, invited the prior and two monks to dine with him.

. The invitation was accepted, in such a manner as to lull every suspicion, the monks sat down to table and ate and drank plentifully with their guests, who after the repast thanked them heartily for their hospitality, upon which the prior rose and said: Gentlemen, if you have any worldly affairs to settle, there is no time to be lost; this is the last meal you and I shall take on earth, in an hour we shall know the secrets of the world to come.

The prior and his two monks had put a deadly poison into the wine, in which they had pledged the

French officers, and notwithstanding the antidotes immediately given by the doctors, in less than an hour every man, hosts and guests had ceased to live.

Conversation.

Questions.	Answers.
Where did a regiment of the guard of Jerome ex-king of Westphalia arrive?	*The regiment arrived under the walls of Figueiras.*
When did that happen?	*During the wars of Napoleon in Spain.*
What message did the general send?	*He sent a message to the prior to demand, if he would prepare any refreshments for his officers and men.*
What did the prior reply?	*The prior replied, that the men would find good quarters in the town, but that he etc.*
Did he do so?	*Yes, he did, for about an hour afterwards, a plentiful dinner was served.*
What did the general know?	*The general knew, by experience, how necessary it was for the French to be on their guard, when eating and drinking with Spaniards, lest they be deceived.*
What did he do then?	*He invited the prior and two monks to dine with him.*

Was the invitation accepted?	Yes it was, and in such a manner as to lull every suspicion
How did the monks behave?	They sat down to table, ate and drank plentifully with their guests
What did these guests do after the repast?	They thanked the monks heartily for their hospitality.
But what did the prior say to them?	He rose and said: Gentlemen, if you have any wordly affairs to settle etc.
What had the prior and the monks put into the wine?	They had put a deadly poison into the wine, in which they had pledged the French officers.

Ripetizione.

In-quali casi si mette l'aggettivo dopo il nome? Quale ufficio fa il participio presente innanzi ai nomi? Come si formano gli aggettivi composti? Quand' è che le parti del corpo van precedute dall'articolo definito? Ditemi l'infinito, passato e participio passato del verbo *nascondere*.

Lezione trentesima ottava. Lesson the thirty eighth.

SINTASSI E PARTICOLARITÀ DEI PRONOMI.

289.

Il pronome personale non si ripete avanti a più verbi di seguito anche so separati dalla congiunzione *and*.

He drinks and smokes the whole day, Beve e fuma tutto il giorno.

I pronomi e aggettivi dimostrativi e possessivi non stanno mai uniti.

This book of mine, questo mio libro.

Il pronome relativo *that* che abbiamo veduto di uso facoltativo per le persone animali e cose, si deve usare nei seguenti casi:

1° Quando i nomi antecedenti a cui si riferisce rappresentano persone e cose o animali:

L'uomo e il cane che corrono, *The man and dog that run.*

2° Dopo l'interrogativo *who?*
3° Dopo il superlativo:

Siete la donna più bella che io abbia mai visto. *You are the prettiest woman that I ever saw.*

4° Dopo la parola *same:*

He is the same, that blamed you yesterday.

That non può essere preceduto da alcuna preposizione, essa vien posta dopo:

Il paese del quale parlate, *The country that you speak of.*

Con *who* e *which* la preposizione si può metter tanto prima che dopo.

To *judge*, giudicare *to contribute*, contribuire
infatuated, fatuo *improvement*, miglioramento
to console, consolare *army*, armata.

That friend of yours that you spoke me of so often and who has left Turin in the year 1865, has returned from his travels. How do you know this? I saw him yesterday evening at Mr. Betti's, the same that I have introduced you to. Has he become a wise man by his travelling? I could'nt exactly tell you, because I have spoken very little with him, he drank and played the whole evening, but if I were to judge from his behaviour and a little story he told us, I think him the same fool that you spoke me of, and the most infatuated young man that I ever knew. It appears then, that the men and things that he has studied have not much contributed to the improvement of his mind. — Who that does'nt know that middle-sized bad-looking gentleman, would think him to be the most gallant general that ever commanded an army? The physician, whom you have sent me for, is not to be found, send for another. Have you received any news from Mr. Belli? Since he left home six months ago we have received no news from him. Did he leave any relation home? Yes, he has left two brothers and one sister.

290.

Avete udito la triste nuova? Povero me, mi spaventate, non ho udito nulla, che c'è? L'officiale di stato maggiore, quel mio amico al quale vi ho presentato, quello stesso che ci fece servire un abbondante pranzo quando lo andammo a visitare. . . . Ebbene? . . . Egli è morto jer l'altro. Che peccato! Mi si dice che fosse il più valoroso officiale di stato maggiore che fosse nell'armata ed uomo d'ingegno. Lasciò figli? Sì, signore, egli lasciò moglie e due figli. Egli aveva viaggiato molto, e gli uomini e le cose che egli accuratamente aveva studiato, avevano contribuito al miglioramento della sua mente. Sono andato a visitare sua moglie e ho tentato di consolarla. — Questa mia penna non è buona a nulla, ditemi di grazia dove comperate quelle vostre penne, delle quali mi avete tanto parlato, e che voi dite sono le migliori che vi sieno in Firenze? Le compro da un libraio che dimora vicino a me. Quello stesso dal quale avete comperato quel libro così interessante? Lo stesso; io vi consiglio di andare da lui, perché è il mercante più onesto che io abbia mai conosciuto. — Chi potendo (il quale potesse) sposarvi preferirebbe rimaner celibe? Solo un pazzo. Chi, essendovi vicino non si innamorerebbe di voi? Solo un cieco. — Perché mi lasciate solo? Ho molti affari e non posso restare più a lungo, ho lasciato mio fratello molto ammalato e devo andare a trovarlo.

291.

Il pronome *Lo* quando fa le veci d'un aggettivo si volge in inglese colla parola *so*:

Voi siete diligente oggi, perché non lo siete sempre?   *You are diligent to-day, why are you not always so?*

Si volge pure colla parola *so* nelle frasi affermative e col pronome *it* nelle interrogative e negative quando esso è accompagnato da uno dei verbi seguenti:

to suppose, supporre
to hope, sperare
to believe, credere

to say } dire.
to tell }

Coi verbi ausiliari non si traduce.

the bill of lading, la polizza di carico
to forward my interests, promuovere i miei interessi
situation, impiego   *likely*, probabilmente.

I took the liberty to call on you in ordre to request your company for some days at our country. I thank you heartily, you are a very good and obliging young man, but your brother is not so, and I do not like to meet with him. He thinks himself the wisest man on the earth. Is he really? I do not think it, people that are wise in their own opinion, you know, are seldom so in that of others. Shall you go to Leghorn this year? I hope so. Shall there be many of our friends? I suppose so. Did your brother find the bill of lading that he was looking for? I do not believe it. Yes, he has found the bill of lading but it is of no use to him. Why then? I don't know he says so. Are those books of any use to you? Yes, they are. — I am generally satisfied with your brother's compositions, but never was, nor ever shall be, with yours. — If you will forward my interests, when you go to Paris, I'll forward yours, when I go to London. I am likely to set off to morrow evening. If I may be of any use to you during your absence, you may dispose of me. I thank you but I am likely to be back in a week or two. Try to find a situation for my poor nephew, you'll oblige him very much. I'll try, but it is very difficult to find a situation for a young man in such bad times, you know.

292.

È vero che vostro fratello sposerà la bella Carlotta? Egli lo spera ma io non lo credo. Credete che il padre di lei abbia qualche obbiezione a questo matrimonio? Lo suppongo. E perchè lo supponete? Perchè egli è ricco, e mio fratello non lo è. Egli lo può divenire, è giovane d'ingegno ed ama il lavoro. Speriamolo. — Ho ricevuta la polizza di carico ma non mi serve a nulla perchè le merci non sono ancora arrivate. Inclusa vi mando la polizza di carico, spero che le merci saranno di già arrivate e che potrete venderle subito, se non lo sono, scrivetemelo. State in guardia, egli è uno scroccone. Perchè me lo dite? Per timore ch'egli v'inganni. Scusate, ma non lo credo, egli ha sempre promosso i miei interessi, e ha trovato un eccellente impiego a mio cognato. Io credo che egli ha promosso i vostri interessi per ingannarvi più facilmente; vedrete probabilmente che ho ragione.

293.

——, February 18th, 18—.

Dear ——,—When you left ——, you were kind enough to promise, that should it be in your power to forward my interests in any manner, you would feel a pleasure in so doing. I am now in want of a situation, my former employer having sold his business, (*) and his successor having, as he informs me, a sufficient number of hands for all the work he is likely to have. If, therefore, you should hear of any situation or employment which you consider likely to suit me, either in my own business, that of a ——, or in any other in which I can make myself useful, your recommendation would greatly oblige, and be of material service to,

Dear——,

Yours very truly,

To Mr. Baroni, Esq. (**) (——).

294.

to be about, essere in procinto
such as, quale (indica la qualità)
overjoyed, fuori di sè dalla gioia

(*) ceduto il suo commercio
(**) Abbreviazione di *Esquire* è titolo tra Signore e Cavaliere, si usa negli indirizzi di lettere a persone civili, e si metta dopo il nome p. e.: Al signor Vanni, *To Mr. Vanni Esq.*

acknowledgment, dichiarazione — *necklace*, collana
to require, esigere — *in the meanwhile*, frattanto
to make choice, far scelta — *to trust*, aver fiducia
the trust, la fiducia — *trunk*, baule
to draw, tirare, trarre — *drew   drawn*
to withdraw, ritirarsi — *withdrew withdrawn*

What are you about to do? I am about to set out for England, have you a trunk to lend me? I have a very ugly one, but such as it is, it is at your service. Will you be so kind as to lend me also ten pounds? Here it is (*). I am much obliged to you, do you require a written acknowledgment? It is not necessary, I trust you. Go to Mr. Marchesim's and make choice of a fine necklace. Will you give me the money to pay it? Never mind, he knows me and has trust in me, tell him he may draw upon me for the sum. He withdrew from business because he was too old. He required a written acknowledgment because he did not trust me. Go and write to your father the good news, I am sure he will be overjoyed, in the meanwhile I go and make choice of some fine present to send to my daughter. He had drawn upon me for fifty pounds but I did non accept the bill. In the meanwhile the barber drew his comb and razor from his pocket. — A sailor was drawn out of the water.

295.

Sono stato questa mattina a visitare vostro cognato, era fuori di sé dalla gioia per causa di una buona novella che egli ha ricevuto; egli era in procinto di partire e mi pregò di far scelta di qualche libro per regalarmelo. Egli pensa di ritirarsi dagli affari perchè è divenuto ricco. Io mi sono ritirato da tre anni. Egli non

---

(*) Il pronome che si riferisce a summe di denaro è sempre al singolare.

volle ritirarsi perchè sperava di diventar più ricco. Egli si ritirò vergognosamente quando i suoi amici avevano bisogno di lui. Mandatemi il vostro fattore con la somma che mi avete promessa. Non posso mandarvi il mio fattore con la somma perchè non mi fido di lui. E perchè lo tenete? Perchè quale egli è, è migliore di molti altri. Se voi esigete una dichiarazione scritta son pronto a farvela. La carrozza era tirata da quattro bei cavalli, ma nonostante non potè arrivare in tempo. Se siete mancante di denaro traete sopra di me e frattanto pregate il vostro amico di prestarvi ciò che abbisognate. Che cosa c'è in quel baule? Esso è pieno di collane che devo mandare a Parigi.

296.

to entrust, confidare
witness, testimonio
to violate, violare
thankfulness, gratitudine
to hurry, affrettarsi
to dupe { ingannare
uccellare

fully, completamente
to carry, portare
to restore, restituire
the performance, l'adempimento
the breach, violazione
to be the dupe, esser vittima
astonishment, stupore.

THE BITER BIT. (*).

A merchant in the East, being about to set out on a journey, entrusted a dervise, whom he thought his friend, with a purse of gold. Being fully convinced of his probity, he did not require a written acknowledgment for the deposit. On his return he applied to him for his money, but the perfidious dervise denied having received any. The exasperated merchant complained to the cadi of Bagdad, who, seeing that the want of witnesses and written documents would make a decision extremely

(*) Il morditore morso.

difficult, ordered the merchant to call again on the following day, and immediately sent for the unfaithful dervise.

The cadi received him with civility, and after some conversation: An affair of consequence, said he, obliges me to leave the country for some time; I have a very considerable sum of gold that I dare not carry with me; I make choice of you as a depositary, because I do not know in this city another man more honest. Do not speak of the affair, and I will send you the money to-morrow-night. The dervise, overjoyed, assured the cadi of his inviolable fidelity, and returned home, no doubt fully determined to violate it. The merchant did not fail to call upon the cadi next day, who, as soon as he saw him: go to your dervise, said he, and if he refuses to restore the charge left to him, threaten him that you will complain to me. He instantly obeyed, and the dervise hearing the name of the cadi, whose confidence he had so much interest to preserve, delivered him the trust. The merchant returned to the cadi, informed him of the result, and expressed his thankfulness for the favour.

In the meanwhile the dervise waited impatiently for the performance of the promise the cadi had made him, and alarmed at hearing no news of it, he hurried to him, but what was his astonishment, when he heard himself reproached by the judge for his breach of faith! He withdrew in great confusion and despair, for having been the dupe of his own credulity.

Conversation.

Questions.	Answers.
What was a merchant in the East about?	*He was about to set out on a journey.*
What would he entrust?	*He would entrust a purse of gold.*

Whom would he entrust with it?	A dervise whom e thought his friend.
Why did he not require a written acknowledgment for the deposit?	Because he was fully convinced of the dervise's probity.
Did the dervise give him his money, when on his return he applied to him for it?	No, he did not, he rather denied having received any.
What did then the exasperated merchant do?	He complained to the cadi of Bagdad.
Could the cadi help immediately?	No, he could not.
Why?	Because of the want of witnesses etc.
What did he do then?	He ordered the merchant to call again on the following day, and immediately sent for the unfaithful dervise.
How did the cadi receive him?	He received him with civility.
What did he say to him?	An affair of consequence etc.
What then dared he not carry with him?	A sum of gold.
Why did he make a choice of the dervise as a depositary?	Because, said he, he did not know in the city another man more honest.
Of what did the dervise assure the cadi?	He assured the cadi of his inviolable fidelity, and returned home, no doubt fully determined to violate it.
Did the merchant call upon the cadi next day?	Yes, he did not fail to do so.
What did the cadi say to him?	Go to your dervise, etc.
Did the merchant do so?	Yes, he did.

What did the dervise do on hearing the name of the cadi?	He delivered him the trust, having much interest to preserve the cadi's confidence.
Where did then the merchant go to?	He returned to the cadi, informed him of the result, and expressed his thankfulness for the favour.
What did the dervise do in the meanwhile?	He waited impatiently for the performance of the promise the cadi had made him.
Where did he go to?	Hearing no news of the promise, he hurried to the cadi.

Ripetizione.

Quand'è che si elide il pronome personale? Come si traduce: *questa mia penna?* Perchè si traduce così? In quali casi si deve adoperare il pronome relativo *that?* Come si traduce il pronome *to?* Verbi irregolari, *tirare, tirai, tirato; ritirarsi, mi ritirai, ritirato.*

Lezione trentesima nona. Lesson the thirty ninth.

CONTINUAZIONE

DELLA SINTASSI E PARTICOLARITÀ DEI PRONOMI

297.

Il pronome impersonale *si* è reso in inglese col passivo del verbo, cioè cambiando l'oggetto in soggetto, quando nella frase italiana il soggetto non ha alcuna importanza:

Dove si vendono i migliori libri ? — *Where the best books are sold ?*

costui, colui, costei, colei, non avendo corrispettivi in inglese si rendono con :

this { *fellow / man*
this { *girl / woman*
costoro { *these men / these women*

that { *fellow / man*
that { *girl / woman*
coloro { *those men / those women*

either, l'uno o l'altro
neither, nè l'uno nè l'altro
to court, corteggiare
to deal (*) { trattare / agire *dealt dealt*
to bid, ordinare *bade, bid* o *bidden*
star, stella

franckness, franchezza
to take a drive, fare una passeggiata in carrozza
to have to deal, aver a fare a *bankrupt*, un fallito
not even, nemmanco.

(*) L'*ea* nei verbi irregolari si pronuncia *i* lungo nell'infinito e nel presente, *e* chiuso nel passato e participio passato.

I should want a new coat, but I don't know where to go and by one; could you tell me where the best coats are sold? Let us go and see in Tornabuoni street, I am told the finest coats are sold there. — That girl is courted by two of your friends, do you know, whom she shall prefer? Perhaps neither. Why then? I dare say she does'nt like either. — Bid that man to go about his business I have nothing to deal with him. Why are you angry with him? I am not angry at all, but I can't bear that fellow, what displeases me about him, is his want of frankness; he told me he has plenty of money, and I hnow what money he has inherited is already spent. — I am at a loss, what to begin, to pass this tiresome evening. Let us go and take a drive to the colli. Are you fool? Don't you see it is a dark evening, not even a star is to be seen; I like to walk or to take a drive in the evening, when the moon and the stars shine in heaven. — About what where you speaking with that man? About business of great importance. Do you know what kind of man you have to deal with? He has dealt with me with great franckness, that is the reason why I rely upon him. Take care he is either a bankrupt or a pick-pocket. I do not believe it. Nor I neither, did, before he had cheated me.

298.

Ditemi di grazia, dove si può trovar buona carta, ho molte lettere da scrivere, e la carta che avevo fu bruciata dal figlio del mio padron di casa. Che peccato ; buona carta, buone penne e buon inchiostro si trova dal libraio Paggi. — Non posso sopportare costui, ditegli che vada via, egli ha trattato con me vergognosamente. Badate con chi avete a fare. Costui ha trattato con me senza franchezza, non voglio aver a fare con lui, per timore d'essere ingannato. Ciò che costei ha fatto, merita il disprezzo d'ogni uomo onesto. Vi fidereste di quell'uomo? No davvero. Nemmeno io. Sono i vostri due cugini in casa? Avrei bisogno di parlare con uno o con l'altro. L'uno e l'altro sono usciti, per quest'oggi non potrete parlare nè con l'uno nè con l'altro. Ordinate a vostro figlio di agire con maggior franchezza. Ha egli mai agito senza franchezza? Si davvero, e inoltre mi dispiace in lui quella presunzione con cui tratta con i suoi compagni. Vi piace passeggiar in carrozza? Moltissimo, ogni domenica faccio una passeggiata in carrozza alle cascine.

209.

every, ogni

each { ogni / ognuno / ciascuno } a differenza di *every*, *each* sta anche senza il nome inoltre esso ha un senso distribuitivo che manca a *every*.

veruno, nessuno, niuno { *nobody anybody* (per le persone) / *none, not any* / *no one* } persone e cose

nobody, no one fanno le veci di sostantivi p. e.:

Nobody thinks himself ignorant

none, not any, not one seguiti da preposizione innanzi ai sostantivi:

I saw none of your friends

to remit, rimettere *herein contained*, qui accluso
all is over with me, la è finita per me
to inquire about some one, chieder notizie di qualcuno
to fail, fallire.

Every thing must come to an end. Each passion speaks a different language. Necessity makes something of every thing. Nobody thinks himself ignorant except the wise. I am told Mr. Ferrutti has failed, is it true? Yes but do not tell it to any body, he hopes to settle his business again. When I entered all the members of the comittee were present; each recomended a different remedy.

Here you are my dear friend, I did not know that you were arrived. No one has seen me, and I have seen nobody. And why did you hide yourself? Because I have many friends and if they knew I was here every one would have called on me and I cannot lose the little time I have necessary for my business. Nobody shall succeed in puzzling me because I do not trust to any body. I am at a loss how to pass the time. Why do you not read any musing book? I have none. All is over with me I am abandoned by every body, each of my friends has refused to come in my help. Some give me fair words other do not even pity me. — I remit you heiren contained my portrait but no one of your friends must know it. He has remitted me a lettere for you, but I could'nt find you, I have inquired about you to all your friends, every one told me you were not in town.

300.

di costì, *of our place*   di costà, *of your place*
sfuggire, *to avoid*   chiunque, *whoever*.

Signore vi rimetto qui acclusa la polizza di carico delle merci che mi avete commesso, se ho dimenticato qualcosa compiacetevi di darmi pronta notizia, che vi spedirò il tutto al più presto possibile; frattanto ho tratto sopra di voi per l'ammontare del vostro debito. Ho inteso da qualche amico che i signori Franceschi e C.° di costà, hanno fallito, ditemi se la notizia è vera.— La è finita per me, dacchè sono diventato povero, niuno mi ama, tutti mi disprezzano ed odiano, quando era ricco tutti i miei amici erano sempre attorno a me, adesso tutti mi lasciano solo, ciascuno mi sfugge, niuno ha pietà di me.— Se avessi qualche amico a Parigi andrei molto volontieri a passarvi qualche tempo. Io ne ho alcuni colà se volete vi presenterò ad essi. — Siccome ho la chiave d'un palco per questa sera, son venuto a vedere se volete venir al teatro. Molto volentieri. Ma non avete tempo da perdere. Subito, aspettatemi un momento, vado a vestirmi, frattanto potete far scelta di qualche libro e leggere. Non mi piace alcuno dei vostri libri sono troppo noiosi; andate fate presto, vi aspetto. — Giovanni, ha chiesto nessuno mie notizie quest'oggi? No signore, nessuno è venuto quest'oggi a chiedere vostre notizie. Chiunque venga, direte che non sono in casa.

301.

fare un contratto, *to make a bargain*
di mestiere, *by trade*
fabbro ferraio, *blacksmith*
visitare esaminare, *to view*
recarsi a, andar a trovare, *to wait upon*
qualunque \ *whatever* (innanzi a sostantivo)
per quanto / *however* (*) (innanzi ad aggettivo).

vantarsi; *to pride one's self*
isola, *island (ailand)*
scappare, *to make off*

Ho fatto un contratto con un tale fabbro-ferraio di mestiere, e me ne vanto perchè sono sicuro di guadagnar molto con esso. È esso un abile fabbro-ferraio? Mi si dice, che è il più abile nell'isola, e se ne vanta. Qualcuno però mi dice che ce n'è uno più abile. Ce n'era ma era pieno di debiti e fu costretto di scappar dall'isola. Per quanto briccone egli sia, e qualunque sforzo egli faccia non riuscirà ad ingannarmi. Dopo aver fatto un cattivo contratto e aver perduto tutto il suo, scappò e per quanti sforzi i suoi abbiano fatto non sono riusciti a scoprire dove si è nascosto. Prima di scappare egli si era recato da me e m'aveva pregato di prestargli cento lire, ma io gliele rifiutai perchè sapeva che per quanto onesto fosse non poteva rendermele. Ho esami-

---

(*) Il soggiuntivo che segue *whoever, whatever, however*, si traduce col mezzo dell'ausiliario *may*.

nato accuratamente la merce che mi avete spedita e il prezzo corrente che avete accluso nella vostra del 17 corrente (*) e sono costretto a rimandarvi la merce perché non mi conviene. Domani alle 5 mi recherò da voi per fare il contratto del quale abbiamo parlato la settimana passata, frattanto compiacetevi di esaminare il prezzo corrente che troverete qui sotto. Non vi vantate tanto di tale affare, se egli scappa, siete rovinato. Per quanto ricco egli sia non è mai contento.

302.

to hit upon, trovare, venir in mente
naked, nudo
stout, forte
hand-bills, manifesti a mano
recollection, memoria
pursuit, ricerca, inseguimento.
to strip, spogliare
dealer, commerciante
newly, nuovamente da poco tempo
previous, prima
to make amends, risarcire

CURIOUS EXPEDIENT.

Two Irishmen, blacksmiths by trade, went to Jamaïca. Finding soon after their arrival, they could do nothing without a little money to begin with, but that, with sixty or seventy pounds and industry, they might be able to do some business, they hit upon the following ingenious expedient. One of them stripped himself naked, and the other made him black from head to foot. This being done, he took him to one of the negro-dealers, who, after viewing and approving his stout athletic appearance, made a bargain to pay eighty pounds for him and prided himself on the purchase, supposing him to be one of the finest negroes on te island. The same evening this newly

(*) *Instant* in abbreviazione *inst*.

manufactured negro made off to his countryman, washed himself clean, and resumed his former appearance. Rewards were in vain offered in hand-bills, pursuit was eluded, and discovery, by care and caution, was made impossible. The two Irishmen with the money commenced business and succeeded so well, that they returned to England with a fortune of several thousand pounds. Previous however to their departure from the island, they waited upon the gentleman from whom they had received the money, recalled the circumstance of the negro to his recollection and made amends both for principal and interest with thanks.

Conversation.

Questions.	Answers.
Who went to Jamaica?	*Two Irishmen.*
What were they?	*They were blacksmiths by trade.*
What did they find soon after their arrival?	*They found, they could do nothing without a little money to begin with.*
With how much did they think to be able to get on?	*They thought that, with sixty or seventy pounds and industry they might be able to do some business.*
What did they do then?	*They hit upon an ingenious expedient.*
What was that expedient?	*One of them stripped himself naked.*
And the other?	*The other made him black from head to foot.*
To whom did he take him then?	*He took him to a negro-dealer.*

Did the negro-dealer view him?	Yes, he did and he approved his stout athletic appearance.
How much did he pay for him?	He made a bargain to pay eighty pounds for him.
On what did he pride himself?	He prided himself on the purchase, supposing him to be one of the finest negroes on the island.
What did the newly manufactured negro do the same evening?	He made off to his countryman, washed himself clean, and resumed his former appearance.
What was offered then?	Rewards were offered in hand-bills.
Did the pursuit succeed?	No, it was eluded, and discovery, by care and caution, was made impossible.
What did the Irishmen do with the money?	They commenced business.
Did they succeed in it?	Yes, they succeeded so well that they returned to England with a fortune of several thousand pounds.
Upon whom did they wait before their departure from the island?	Previous to their departure from the island, they waited upon the gentleman from whom they had received the money.
What circumstance did they recal to his memory?	They recalled to his memory the circumstance of the negro.
Did they pay him anything?	Yes, they made amends both for principal and interest with thanks.

lip l'zione.

Verbi irregolari *trattare, trattai, trattato, ordinare, ordinai, ordinato.* Come si rendono in inglese I pronomi: *costui, colui, costei, colei, costoro, coloro?* Che differenza passa tra *each* e *every?* Come si rende, *nessuno, ntuno,* nei diversi casi di loro applicazione? Come si traduce *chiunque, qualunque, per quanto?*

Lezione quarantesima.   Lesson the fortieth.

SINTASSI E PARTICOLARITÀ DEL VERBO.

303.

Si suole elidere il segno verbale *shall will should would* ecc.) dinnanzi a più verbi che si succedono alla medesima persona, numero, tempo o modo, p. e.:

I will court and marry her, la corteggerò e la sposerò.

Si adopera l'ausiliare *do* e *did* anche nelle frasi affermative quando si vuol dare maggior forza alla frase, p. e.:

Do listen to me, ascoltatemi.

Non si adopera l'ausiliare *do* neanche nelle frasi interrogative e negative: col verbi difettivi, dopo il pronome interrogativo *who?* quand'è soggetto; e dopo i verbi *to dare* e *to need*, p. e.:

Who cries? chi piange   *I dare not*, non oso.

underneath, qui sotto
buyer, (*) compratore
by return of post
treasure, tesoro
to be advanced, crescer, alzar (del prezzo)
xix
judge, giudice

described, descritto
shortly, in breve
a volo di posta
a volta di corriere
the current prices, prezzi correnti
apprehension, apprensione, timore

subjoined, unito, aggiunto, sottoposto.

(*) Da *to buy*, comperare, si formano molti sostantivi da verbi, colla aggiunta della desinenza *er*.

I am in a great apprehension, do answer me by return of post that I may know the truth as soon as possible. — You are a soldier and fear death? I confess I do fear it, but for others not for myself. — Underneath you will find the current prices of the articles you have subjoined in your last, but do send your orders by return of post, because there are plenty of buyers, and who knows if the prices are not shortly to be advanced? — Who writes your english letters so well? I need not tell you, because you know as well as I. I suppose but I dare not say, lest I be mistaken. — Your teacher told me that you will shortly read speak and write english as well as I. I dare not hope it. Why do you not listen to me? I beg your pardon, I do listen to you with great attention. — Who dirties your books? It is my little child. Do chide him otherwise he will dirty, spoil and tear all your books. I have already chidden it, but never mind, I do study also with spoiled books. — « I do not hnow how ot judge the present case, » said an ignorant judge. One of the present observed. « Do you think the king is to pay your ignorance? » I do not « replied he » the king pays me and well for what I do know; were he to pay me for what I do not know, all his treasures would not suffice.

304.

Mandatemi deh, a volo di posta, il prezzo corrente degli articoli qui sotto descritti, mi dicono vi sono molti compratori, e sto alquanto in apprensione che i prezzi alzino in breve. — Mi capite se parlo adagio? Non avete bisogno di parlare adagio io vi capisco anche se parlate presto. Osate forse dire che sapete l'inglese meglio. di me e che non avete bisogno di studiarlo di più? Non oso dir ciò, ma chi sa se in breve non saprò meglio di voi, e frattanto vi dico che vi capisco benissimo. Chi vi scrive che siete fuori di voi dalla gioia? È mio zio che in breve verrà e mi porterà seco in campagna dove giocherò e mi divertirò senza essere sgridato. — Se voi esigete una dichiarazione, scrivetemelo e ve la manderò a volo di posta, ma mi rincrescerebbe che non vi fidaste di me. Avete torto mio caro, io mi fido di voi e nondimeno esigo una dichiarazione scritta, per tutti i casi che possono accadere. — Se i prezzi non sono alzati potete mandarmi subito gli articoli qui sotto descritti. Chi sgrida quel povero ragazzo? Nessuno lo sgrida ora, io lo sgridai perchè non mi ascoltava, e oso dire lo avreste sgridato anche voi.

305.

Quando due verbi al futuro sono accompagnati da voci di tempo il primo si volge in inglese al presente p. e.:

When I see him I will give   Quando lo vedrò gli darò la
him your letter,   vostra lettera.

Ietessamente nelle frasi di proporzione il primo verbo si mette al presente, p. e.:

the sooner you come the bet-   quando più presto vorrete
ter you shall see,   tanto meglio vedrete.

to breed, allevare, educare   *bred   bred*
the retail price, il prezzo al minuto, di dettaglio
to be worth a sum of money, possedere una somma di danaro
XVII
by the by, a proposito   *the purchase,* la compra,
to admit of, dar luogo a   l'acquisto
to retire, ritirarsi   *to increase,* accrescere.

As soon as I receive the current prices I will order the purchase of the articles we have spoken about. Please send me also the retail price that I may see the profit those goods admit of. The more carefully you bring up your children the less misfortunes will they cause you through life. When will you retire from trade? As soon as I am worth one hundred thousand pounds, I will retire from trade. How much do you gain a year? Not very much now. Then you want at least thirty years to retire from trade. No, because the larger my capital is the faster it will increase. — Vell-bred children ought to obey their parents and teachers. Who insulted you? That ill bred man. What is he? He was a merchant, but now he has retired from trade and as he is worth some thousand pounds he is as proud as the emperor of China. By the by, did you order many purchases to be made at Paris? No because the little difference between the current prices and the retail ones does not admit of any profit.

306.

Subito che saprete bene l'inglese avrete un buon posto in commercio. Non ho bisogno di posti perchè posseggo diecimila lire sterline e posso vivere delle mie rendite. Quanto più accrescerete il vostro capitale tanto meglio potrete educare i vostri figli e tanto più sarete felice, poichè figli bene educati sono la gioia dei loro genitori. A proposito vi ho portato il prezzo di dettaglio che mi avete chiesto, se credete che esso dia luogo a qualche profitto, compiacetevi di dirmelo, poichè subito che mio figlio sarà a Londra gli scriverò di fare delle compere. A proposito è vero che vostro cognato si è ritirato dal commercio e che possiede più di venti mila lire sterline? Lo dicono ma non lo credo, quando lo vedrò glielo domanderò. A proposito quanto credete che posseda il signor Leoni? Egli voleva far delle compre nella mia bottega, ma siccome nun aveva denaro con sè, io non mi son fidato di lui e non gli ho venduto nulla. Avete fatto male egli possiede più di cinque mila lire. Compiacetevi signore di mandarmi le mille lire che mi dovete a saldo dei nostri conti, perchè i miei affari non danno più luogo a profitto e io desidero di ritirarmi.

307.

Sir

I request you will be so kind, by return of post, as to let me know the curren prices of the articles which I have subjoined. If I think they admit of sufficient profit, you will shortly receive a very considerable order for myself and correspondents.

I am, Sir, you humble servant.
(The list follows).

308.

Risposta:

Conforme alla vostra domanda ho aggiunto qui sotto, il prezzo degli articoli di cui mi parlate; vi mostro nello stesso tempo anche i prezzi acciocchè possiate giudicare dei profitti. Siccome ho qualche timore che il loro prezzo in breve sia per alzare, io vi raccomando il tempo presente come il migliore per far compre.

309.

it will do, basterà, faràal vostro caso
to be pleased, esser contento
sovereing, sovrana

disposal, disposizione
upon the whole, al postutto
crown, scudo.

I come to beg a service of you. I am at your disposal. Can you lend me ten pounds? I have not so much money as that about me. But if you will come home with me, you shall have it. I will not give you that trouble. It will be no trouble at all. No, no; I can do without it. Let me see how much I have about me.

Here's a five pound note, a sovereing, and three crowns. Will that do? I think it will. I will return it to you before the end of the month. When you please. Now you must do me anocher service, Dispose of me. Here are different things which your neighbour has sold me, and I want to take your opinion of them. He promised to take them back, if I found them too dear. How much does this cost you? Tvo pounds ten. (*) It is too much. You must not give more than two pounds for it. And this? Eighteen shillings. Are you sure of it? Yes, certain. It is very cheap indeed. It makes amends for the price of the other. Here is a tea-table, for which he asks three pounds there is nothing to say to that. It is the price I paid for mine. So, upon the whole, you think it is not too dear? No, indeed. You may trust my neighbour; he is a very honest fellow.

310.

crescere) *to grow*   *grew*   *grown*
diventare)
adirarsi, *to grow angry*   gota, guancia, *cheek*
zuccheriera, *sugar-basin*   ingoiare, *to swallow*
provvedere di, *to supply*   piattello, sottocoppa, *saucer*
servizio di porcellana, *set of china*.

Guardate che bel servizio di porcellana; dove lo avete comperato? A Firenze da Ginori, ma esso è sciupato perchè il mio bambino ruppe due sottocoppe. Quando andrò a Firenze vedrò se posso riuscire a trovarne eguali a queste e ve le manderò. Mi obbligherete moltissimo. L'ho provveduto di tutto ciò che gli abbisognava e nondimeno si adira contro di me perchè vorrei che si sbarazzasse dei cattivi amici che ha attorno. Avete le guancie

---

(*) *due lire e dieci scellini*, la parola *shilling* si usa elidere, in tali casi.

rosse, vi siete adirato con qualcuno? Mi sono adirato col mio servo che ha rotto due sottocoppe e una zuccheriera. Perchè non vi disfate di un tal servo? Vorrei disfarmene ma non so come fare, tuttavia subito che ne troverò un altro mi disfarò di lui. Dacchè è diventato ricco non si cura più dei suoi vecchi amici. Badate, il vostro ragazzo romperà quella sottocoppa e allora il servizio di porcellana sarà sciupato. Non me ne curo. Con chi vi adirate? Non osodirlo. Perchè non vi servite di zucchero? Non vedete che me ne servo. Non vi piace il te? Anzi mi piace moltissimo; ne ho già ingoiate tre tazze. Dacchè egli è diventato ricco, non è mai più venuto a trovarmi. È cresciuto in superbia più che in ricchezze.

331.

to dip, intingere, tuffare
to prevent, impedire
handsome, (*) bello
concern, riguardo
to apologize, chieder scusa
to tinge { tingere, colorire
peaceably, in pace
to soil, insudiciare
to scream, strillare, gridar forte.

DR. JOHNSON AND MRS. THRALE.

The first time Johnson was in company with Mrs. Thrale, neither the elegance of his conversation, nor the depth of his knowledge could prevent that lady from growing angry at his manners. Among other pieces of indecorum, his tea not being sweet enough, he dipped his fingers into the sugar-basin, and supplied himself with as little ceremony and concern, as if there had not been a lady at table. Every well-bred cheek was tinged with confusion, but Mrs. Thrale was so exasperated that

---

(*) Fa il comparativo e superlativo per eccezione colle terminazioni *er*, *est*.

she ordered the sugar-basin immediately from the table, as if its contents had been contaminated by the Doctor's fingers. The Doctor did not care for it, but peaceably swallowed, as usual, his dozen cups of tea. When he had done, instead of placing his cup and saucer upon the table, he threw them both under the grate, as if he wished to get rid of a devil. The whole table was thrown into confusion. Mrs. Thrale screamed out: Why, Doctor, what have you done? You have spoiled the handsomest set of china I have in the world! — I am very sorry for it, Madam, answered Dr. Johnson apologizing, but I assure you, I did it out of good breeding; for, from your treatment of the sugar-basin, I fancied you would never touch anything again, that I had once soiled with my fingers.

Conversation.

Questions.	Answers.
At what did Mrs. Thrale grow angry?	*She grew angry at Doctor Johnson's manners.*
On what opportunity did she grow angry?	*She grew angry the first time Dr. Johnson was in company with her.*
Which want of decorum was cause of it?	*He dipped his fingers into the sugar-basin.*
Why did he so?	*Because his tea was not sweet enough.*
How did he supply himself?	*He supplied himself with as little ceremony as if there had not been a lady at table.*
What effect did such a behaviour produce?	*Every well-bred cheek was tinged with confusion.*
Was Mrs. Thrale angry?	*Yes, she was so exasperated that ecc.*

Why so?	As if its contents had been contaminated by the Doctor's fingers.
Did the Doctor care for it?	Not at all. but he peaceably swallowed his tea.
How many cups did he drink?	A dozen cups as usual.
When he had done, did he place his cup and saucer upon the table?	No, instead of doing so, he threw them both under the grate, as if he wished to get rid of a devil.
What happened then?	The whole tea-table was thrown into confusion.
What was Mrs. Thrale's exclamation?	Why, Doctor, ecc.
What was the Doctor's reply?	I am very sorry for it, Madam, answered he, but I assure you I did it out of good breeding.
How did he explain that meaning?	From your treatment of the sugar-basin, said he, I fancied you would never touch anything again that I had once soiled with my fingers.

Ripetizione.

Quando si puó elidere il segno verbale? Quando si adopera l'ausiliario *do* anche nelle frase affermative? Quando non lo si adopera nenche nelle negative e interrogative? Quando si usa il presente invece del futuro? Verbi irregolari, *educare, educai, educato; crescere, crebbi, cresciuto.*

Lezione quarantesima prima.   Lesson the forty first.

CONTINUAZIONE
DELLA SINTASSI E PARTICOLARITÀ DEL VERBO.

312.

Le espressioni Italiane *non è vero?, davvero?* si rendono in inglese coll'ausiliare già espresso o sottinteso nella frase antecedente, nella forma esclamativa, interrogativa o interrogativa-negativa secondo il caso p. e.:

Si dice che il Sig. G. è fallito. Davvero?	*I am told M. G. has failed. Has he?*
Verrete a teatro con noi; non è vero?	*You will come to theatre with us; will you not?*
intimate, intimo;	*odd*, strano, ridicolo
to be sure, sicuramente	*I fancy*, m'immagino
to entreat, supplicare	*the brute*, la perfida
$\overset{\text{xv}}{to}$ *kneel*, inginocchiarsi	*knelt knelt.*

Why do you not shake hands with my cousin Julia? you were intimate friends; were you not? To be sure, we were, but we are no more, she is angry with me. Is she? And what is the matter? I must tell you, I had fallen in love with her. Were you? It is very interesting, go on, pray. Well, last saturday, she was alone in her drawing room, I knelt down before her, and declared my passion. Did you? Oh how odd from you, but I fancy you offered your hand at the same time, didn't you? Of course I did, unluckily she refused it. Did she?

I wonder, but why did you kneel? To entreat her. And what did she answer when you knelt down? She laughed heartily. Did she? Oh the brute, I pity you with all my heart. If you do really, you should speak to her for me and try to change her resolution, couldn't you? To be sure, and I will. Tell her, I'll never more kneel before her, but she cannot prevent my adoring (*) her through all my life.

313.

Guardate quel vecchio che s'inginocchia dinnanzi a quella giovane signora, voi lo conoscete, non è vero? M'immagino egli crede di non essere veduto. Certamente. Essa lo burla m'immagino, non è vero? No, v'ingannate essa lo ama. Davvero! Mi meraviglio, quando egli le s'inginocchiò dinnanzi essa rise di cuore. Davvero? Può essere ma io vi assicuro, essa lo ama come un padre.— Inginocchiatevi e domandate perdono. — Vedendo che si adirava gli s'inginocchiò dinnanzi e gli chiese perdono. — Sapete voi il francese? Io so parlar e scrivere francese come un francese. Davvero? A proposito, mi rallegro con voi, vostro padre è diventato molto ricco, non è vero? Vorrei che fosse vero, ma sgraziatamente non è. Se avete tempo potete venire a fare una passeggiata con me, non è vero? Non posso, mio padre non me lo permette. Davvero! Dovreste venirmi a visitare più spesso, non è vero? Non v'adirate, vi prego, non voleva offendervi.

314.

L'infinito italiano soggetto di una proposizione si rende in inglese o coll'infinito o col participio presente, p. e. :

Maritarsi troppo presto è   *To marry too early is*
imprudente.   *imprudent.*

(*) Non può impedirmi di adorarla.

Tirar di scherma di quando — Fencing now and then is in quando è molto salutifero. — very wholesome.

Si adopra l'ausiliare *to be* col participio presente del verbo *to go* per esprimere un'azione che si è o si era in procinto di fare, p. e.:

Sto per partire per la Francia. — *I am going to set out for France.*
Stava per adirarsi contro di me. — *He was going to grow angry with me.*

to borrow, prendere imprestito
to pain, far pena
help, aiuto
melancholy, triste.
to fish, pescare
intelligence, notizia
to turn to, rivolgersi

Could you lend me twenty pounds? Couldn't you? For shame! You are always borrowing. I beg your pardon but borrowing is not stealing. I was going to send him a little note when I met with his servant who told me that he is gone a hunting with some of his friends. He is really too fond of such sports. Yes, hunting and fishing are his favorite pass-time, for my part I prefer reading and writing; for how great is the pleasure of reading!— What are you going to do? I am going to accompany Julia to her dancing-master, if you allow it. I have not the least objection, I am glad that you love your sister, really, to see children well united rejoices a father's heart as much as to see them in discord pains it. But make haste my boy, I am going to set out and I have need of you. Why do you run? Because I am cold, running is the best thing you can do when you are cold. I was going to send him the goods he has committed me, when I received the sad intelligence that he was going to fail, and I know he has no friend to hope any help. Poor fellow, I do pity him with all my heart; not to know where to turn to, nor where to find a friend in need, is indeed a melancholy condition.

315.

Non sapendo come fare per saldare un conto che mi venne presentato, stava per prendere in prestito del danaro dal signor Cocchi, quando mi diede la triste notizia che egli stesso ne aveva gran bisogno perchè uno dei suoi amici stava per fallire, e mi chiese consiglio; io gli dissi: mio caro mi fa pena di vedervi in così triste condizione, e potrei facilmente aiutarvi con un buon consiglio, ma, sapete, dar consigli è facile, ma seguirli è spesso difficile. — Nuotare di quando in quando è molto salutifero ma il tirar di scherma lo è di più. Stava per rivolgermi a mio zio per aiuto quando ricevetti la tristo notizia della sua morte; ora non so a chi rivolgermi, abbiate compassione di me, la mia è una tristissima condizione. — Stava per adirarsi contro di voi, quando nostro padre entrò e chiese scusa per voi. Mi fa pena veder che passate il tempo senza far nulla.

316.

L'infinito italiano che segue il verbo *fare* si rende in Inglese coll'infinito, quando il nome o pronome che lo precede è soggetto dell'infinito, p. e.:

La feci cantare una canzone. *I made her sing a song.*

Si traduce invece col participio passato quando il nome o pronome è oggetto, p. e.:

Le sue virtù la fanno am-   *Her virtues make her ad-*
mirare da ognuno.   *mired by every one.*

Codesta regola s'applica anche agli infiniti che seguono i verbi *to see, to hear, to feel,* coll'avvertenza che se l'infinito esprime una azione continuata, allora invece che coll'infinito lo si rende col participio presente, p. e.:

Vidi ascendere il pallone, *I saw the balloon ascending.*

Il verbo *fare* seguito dall'infinito in senso passivo si rende in oltre col verbi *to get, to have, to cause,* p. e.:

Vi farò punire, *I'll have you punished*

many a (') time, { molte volte *to play,* recitare
{ parecchie „ *murder,* omicidio

player, attore
singer, cantante
to mend, { raccomodare
{ aggiustare.

What do you bring there? I have brought the music that we heard sung yesterday at the count B's and that you liked so much. How kind of you. Have it sung by your daughter whose charming voice all your friends hear with pleasure. You would make me believe that she is a good singer, but you are a flatterer, I know you mistake. Many a time I heard her sing, and I am sure, if you cause her to study, she will grow a first rate singer; ask her singing master and you will hear my words repeated. — Could you make yourself understood if you go to England? I think I could; but I could not make myself understood if I went to France, because I have never learned the french language. To make one's self understood every where, one must study french, because you'll hear it spoken every where. — I'll have those players play something like the murder of my father, said Hamlet. What do you listen to? I hear my neighbour speaking and scolding his servant-maid. I see my wine drunk by my cook, But I saw you also drink many a time. — I have caused my watch to be mended because it went wrong; look what is o'clock by yours. It goes also wrong, I shall have it mended. You must get your books bound othervise they will be quite destroyed. Oh I have got them bound already. One misfortune after another makes me almost despair.

(*) Quando oltre che sulla pluralità, si vuol chiamar l'attenzione anche sopra i singoli suoi componenti, si adopera la frase *many a* e il sostantivo si mette al singolare.

317.

Ho udito parecchie volte cantare la signorina Adelina e vi assicuro che essa ha una voce deliziosa. Mi piace di udirvi parlare così bene di lei. Sento la vostra mano tremare nella mia, che avete? Sono spaventato perchè ho veduto uccidere un povero soldato, vidi pure sua madre piangere vicino a lui; quanto la compiango povera donna! Avete mai veduto recitare il celebre (*) Rossi? Si, parecchie volte. Sentii la sua voce tremare per la paura. Perchè era spaventata? Perchè vide uccidere un uomo nella strada. Davvero? Bisogna che faccia legare i miei libri altrimenti si sciuperanno. Ho fatto fare un paio di stivali e ho fatto raccomodare un paio di scarpe. Fate aggiustare l'orologio, esso ritarda. Vorrei far scrivere a mio figlio una lettera in inglese, ma non posso riuscire. Davvero? Domani mi farò tagliare i capelli perchè fa troppo caldo. Che avete che non potete camminare? Gli stivali mi fanno male. Se li aveste fatti raccomodare, come vi ho detto, non vi farebbero male.

318.

It pains me very much to hear you speaking so badly of one of your intimate friends, and from whom I know many a time you have borrowed money. After having seen him comit a murder I can't feel any friendship for him. The noise you make will cause many a man turn round to see what it is. I don't care. Don't you? but I do. I was going to borrow some money but the cold answer to my first words caused me to speak of something else. I fancy you are going to have your trowsers mended, many a man could take you for a cobbler. Fishing is a very tiresome sport, I prefer hunting. Do you? I fancy you are a good hunter, are you not? I'll have you punished if you don't take more care of your books. I

(*) *celebrated.*

must have them bound, otherwise I can't take any care of them. My dear Julia, you are fond of dancing, I see. It is so amusing, you know. Yes, but it is not very wholesome, many a fair girl is dead for having danced too much, I love you and I would not see you dance so often.

319.

Avete mai udito recitare il Morelli? No signore. Avreste piacere di udirlo recitare? Moltissimo. Subito che vi vedrò studiare come dovreste vi condurrò al teatro. — Stava per prenderle la mano, e inginocchiarmi innanzi a lei quando vidi venire suo padre che la fece andar via con lui. M'immagino che siete innamorato di lei. Molti lo sarebbero se l'avessero udita cantare; essa ha una voce così deliziosa. Davvero! mi meraviglio che suo padre non la faccia cantare in teatro. — Nuotare nell'estate è molto più sano che il ballare. Davvero? È un peccato, perchè mi piace più ballare che nuotare. M'immagino che vi farete pettinare prima di andare al ballo. Certamente. Stava per uscire quando cominciò a piovere e dovetti far venire una carrozza, e per pagarla ho dovuto prendere in prestito cinque franchi dal nipote del mio padron di casa. Davvero? Mi meraviglio!

320.

Fare seguito da un infinito si traduce anche per to bid, *che significa propriamente* ordinare, *e col verbo* to occasion; *si costruisce la frase come col verbo* to cause *eccetto che dopo* to bid *si elide il* to *avanti all'infinito, p. e.:*

Fate salire quell'uomo, *Bid that man come up-stairs.*

salire (le scale), *to go up-stairs*
scendere (le scale), *to go down-stairs*
coltellaccio, *chopper* . scure, *hatchet*

aprire, rompendo, *to break* abbattere colpendo, *to strike down*
open (*)
fucilare
tirare con arma da fuoco } *to shoot shot shot*
sparare

Ordinate alla serva di scendere, che la faccia andare al mercato per comprare un coltellaccio ed una scure. Il ladro stava per aprir la porta rompendola colla scure, quando arrivarono i soldati ed io lo feci arrestare. Scendete dalla vicina e fatevi prestare il coltellaccio. Dite alla signorina Carlotta di salire, che passeremo la sera in buona compagnia. Vi supplico, caro babbo, conducetemi a veder recitare il celebre Salvini, non l'ho mai veduto recitare. Vidi un uomo nel bosco abbattere un albero con un colpo di scure. Lo vedeste voi pure, non è vero? Vedeste mai fucilare un uomo? Parecchie volte quand'era soldato. Tirò sopra di lui e lo feri, non è vero? L'ufficiale comandò di tirare sopra l'inimico. Che cosa aveva commesso il soldato che abbiamo veduto fucilare? Un omicidio. Scendete presto, vedrete passare un uomo che ha commesso un omicidio.

321.

gamekeeper guardaboschi
to drop, lasciar cadere, levarsi
neck, collo
incitement, eccitamento
upper, superiore
shoulder, spalla

to feel for, sentir compassione di
to pace, misurar coi passi
ground, suolo
to demand admittance, chieder permesso di entrare
threat, minaccia.

(*) leggesi *opn*; per regola generale, nella desinenza *en* l'*e* è muta.

FEMALE HEROISM.

Robert, a gamekeeper, residing in a solitary house near Weilheim, had one day gone to church with his family, having caused a daughter of sixteen years of age to stay at home. They had not long been gone, when there appeared, at the door, an old man, apparently half dead with cold. Feeling for his situation, she bid him come in and went into the kitchen to prepare him some soup. Through a window which communicated from the room in which she had left him, she perceived that he had dropped the beard he wore when he entered, and that he now appeared a robust man, and was pacing the room with a poniard in his hand.

Finding no mode of escape, she armed herself with a chopper in one hand, and the boiling soup in the other; and entering the room where he was, first threw the soup into his face, and then struck him a blow on his neck with the hatchet, which brought him insensible to the ground.

At this moment another knock at the door occasioned her to look out of an upper window, when she saw a strange hunter, who demanded admittance, and on her refusal, threatened to break open the door. She immediately took her father's gun, and as he was proceeding to put his threats into execution, she shot him through the right shoulder, on which he made his way back into the forest. Half an hour afterwards, a third person came and asked after an old man who must have passed that way. She said she knew nothing of him; and as he was proceeding to break open the door, having by useless threats endeavoured to prevail upon her to get it opened, she shot him dead on the spot.

The incitement to her courage being now at an end,

her spirits began to sink, and she fired and screamed from the windows, until some persons were attracted to the house, but nothing could induce her to open the door until the return of the family from church.

Conversation.

Questions.	Answers.
What was Robert?	He was a gamekeeper.
Where did he reside?	He resided in a solitary house near Weilheim.
Where had he gone one day with his family?	He had gone to church.
Whom had he caused to stay at home?	He had caused a daughter of sixteen to stay at home.
Who appeared then at the door?	An old man, apparently half dead with cold.
What did she do then?	Feeling for his situation, she bid him come in.
Why did she go into the kitchen?	To prepare him some soup.
What did she perceive then?	She perceived through a window that the man had dropped the beard he wore when he entered.
Through what window did she perceive that?	Through a window which etc.
As what did he appear to her now?	He appeared a robust man.
What was he doing?	He was pacing the chamber with a poniard in his hand.
What did the daughter do when she found no mode of escape?	She armed herself with a chopper in one hand and the boiling soup in the other.

What did she do with that soup?	On entering the room where the man was, she threw that soup into his face.
And afterwards?	She struck him a blow on his neck with the hatchet.
What was the consequence of this blow?	It brought him insensible to the ground.
What occasioned her to look out of the upper window?	Another knock at the door occasioned her to do so.
Whom did she see?	She saw a strange hunter who demanded admittance.
What did he threaten to do, when she refused to open?	He threatened to break open the door.
Did he do so?	Yes, he proceeded to do so.
What did then the daughter do?	She took immediately her father's gun and shot him through the right shoulder.
Who came afterwards?	Half an hour afterwards a third person came.
After whom did that person ask?	The person asked after an old man.
What did she answer?	She said she knew nothing of him.
Did his threats to get the door opened prevail upon her?	No, his threats were useless.
What did she do, when he was proceeding to break open the door?	She shot him dead on the spot.
What was now at an end?	The incitements to her courage were at an end.
What happened then?	The daughter's spirits began to sink, she fired and screamed from the windows.

Ripetizione.

Come si rendono in inglese le espressioni *non è vero?* *davvero!* Come si rende l'infinito soggetto di una preposizione? Come si esprime un' azione che si è o si era in procinto di fare? Come si rende l'infinito italiano che segue il verbo *fare*? A quali altri verbi si applica pure questa regola? Come si rende *fare* innanzi a un infinito in senso passivo? Verbo irregolare: *inginocchiarsi, mi inginocchiai, inginocchiato; fucilare, sparare.*

Lezione quarantesima seconda. Lesson the forty second.

CONTINUAZIONE

DELLA SINTASSI E PARTICOLARITÀ DEI VERBI.

322.

Il passato definito si adopera in inglese soltanto quando l'azione espressa dal verbo è compiuta, e venga indicato un tempo interamente trascorso, p. e.:

Gli scrissi jeri, *I wrote to him yesterday.*

Il passato indefinito o composto si adopera invece: 1° quando il tempo non è indicato, p. e.:

Ho scritto a vostro padre, *I have written to your father.*

2° Quando il tempo indicato non è interamente trascorso, p. e.:

Non ci sono stato quest'anno, *I have not been there this year.*

Quando il verbo al passato imperfetto esprime un'azione che è stata abituale lo si rende in inglese col condizionale volitivo, p. e.:

| Quand'era più giovane mi alzava più di buon'ora. | When (*) younger *I would rise earlier.* |

to admonish, ammonire
to hear from, aver notizie di

farthing, centesimo
sloth, pigrizia
cobbler, ciabattino

to watch, guardare
to be grieved, essere addolorato
bridge, ponte
to spite, sputare.
the eddy, il vortice.

(*) Dopo *when* si usa spesso per eleganza, elidere il verbo *essere*.

Did you hear any thing from Mr. Brunetti? Yes, I have heard from him this week, did he never write to you? Yes, he wrote me last month, but I was in some apprehension as he has been ill, so much the more that when at Paris he would write me once a week. When did you return from bath? I returned the day before yesterday and my family too. What has become of young Francis? He has become a cobbler. How a cobbler? Yes, because his father left him not a farthing in the world, and he was not able to do any thing at all. But how did he pass his early years? When a boy he would for hours stand on a bridge amusing himself by spitting on the water and watching the eddies made by the current. And did his father take care of his education? His father was much grieved at his sloth and would often admonish him, but it was of no use. What are you watching there? There is a boy who spites on the water. I am much grieved at my son's sloth, if he goes on and wastes his time away, I'll leave him nothing at all.

323.

la fattura, *the invoice*	per lo passato, *formerly*
osservare, *to remark*	mercante all' ingrosso, *wholesale merchant*
il braccio, *the ell*	ammonizione, *admonition*,

Ricevetti la fattura delle merci che mi spediste il mese passato, e al più presto possibile vi manderò il denaro, mi permetto frattanto di osservare che per lo passato usavate mandarmi la fattura soltanto dopo tre mesi dalla spedizione delle merci e questa me l'avete spedita dopo un mese. — Che cosa avete fatto questa mattina? Mi sono divertito a stare sul ponte guardando l'acqua e sputando nel fiume. Il maestro era molto addolorato per la sua pigrizia e lo ammoniva spesso. Furono le sue ammonizioni di qualche utilità? No, non servirono a nulla, ed ora che suo padre è morto egli deve fare il ciabattino per vivere. Quanto al braccio avete venduto la tela che compraste la settimana passata dal mercante all'ingrosso? Un franco il braccio. Avete guadagnato molto vendendola al dettaglio? Guadagnai soltanto trenta franchi. — Ho incontrato ieri mattina il vostro scolaro Francesco, quello che sgridavate per la sua pigrizia, il poveretto è in miseria e non sa come fare per guadagnarsi da vivere. Tanto peggio per lui, quando veniva alla scuola egli soleva giuocare invece di far attenzione; si fermava sul ponte più di un'ora, e si divertiva sputando nell'acqua.

324.

Il presente italiano esprimente un'azione o uno stato che ha cominciato da qualche tempo e continua ancora, come nelle frasi:

è un'ora che,   son due anni che,   da un mese

e simili, si rende in inglese o col passato indefinito dell'ausiliare *essere* e il participio presente del verbo principale, p. e.:

Studio inglese da due anni, *I have been studying the english language these two years.*

oppure semplicemente col passato indefinito, ciò che sarebbe specialmente il caso, quando gli ausiliari *essere* ed *avere* sono verbi principali della frase, p. e.:

Siamo qui da un'ora,   *We have been here this hour*
È mezz'ora che gli predico, *I have lectured (o been lecturing) him this half an hour.*

one single, un solo   *to draw*, disegnare
the code, il codice   *to satisfy*, accontentare
to long for, { aspettare, cercare con ansietà
              { desiderare ardentemente

You have been listening to the professor for an hour, could you repeat to me one single word of all that he has said? I couldn't, because I didn't understand him well. How! you have been learning french these nine months and you do not yet understand it? I am afraid you waste your time and money. — I have been longing for you these two hours, there is a German gentleman who cannot make himself understood, please to ask him what he wants. He says he has been at Florence these two months, without meeting with a person speaking his language and that he wants to have these documents translated. — He has consulted the code for one hour and a half, has he found the paragraph in question? — I have lectured the youth for these three hours, but all to no purpose, — Does your daughter draw as well as she sings? She had been learning to draw for one year when her master happened to die. It is a pity, isn't? To be sure, so much so that she made great progresses. Why don't you take another master to cause her to be improved? I have been longing for a good one these three months, but I can't find any; could you recommend me any of your acquaintance? My dear friend I am overjoyed. What is the matter? The solution I have been looking for, to no purpose, for three weeks, I at last found in three minutes. I have been these six weeks in the country, and you have not come once to see me. You ask for your money, I have had it at your disposal for these six months.

325.

Da quanto tempo studiate la lingua tedesca? La s'udio da due anni, ma ancora non la so perfettamente, è una lingua difficile e si deve studiarla almeno tre anni, adesso sono tre mesi che studio pochissimo perchè il mio maestro è partito, sono ansioso di trovarne un altro, potreste indicarmene voi uno buono di vostra conoscenza, non è vero? Procurerò di accontentarvi. — Da quanto tempo siete a Firenze? Sono tre settimane che son a Firenze, vi cerco da quindici giorni perchè desiderava ardentemente di vedervi. Voi educate male il vostro ragazzo, non lo sgridate mai, guardate com'egli è fiero. Son due ore che gli predico di star tranquillo, ma invano. Avete trovato la soluzione del problema che il professore vi ha dato? Son quindici giorni che la cerco inutilmente, non so come fare, alutatemi ve ne prego. Dovreste vergognarvi, studiate matematica da 4 anni e non sapete trovare una soluzione così facile. Son due ore che quel signore inglese parla a vostro padre e che voi lo ascoltate con grande attenzione, potete dirmi ciò che vuole? Non potrei ripetervi una singola parola, non sono che quindici giorni che studio l'inglese.

326.

Will oltre che ausiliare è anche verbo principale, solamente è difettivo, esso non ha che due forme, una per il presente indicativo o una pel passato e condizionale *I will*, io voglio ecc. *I would* ecc. io voleva, volli, vorrei. Per sostituire ai tempi o modi che mancano abbiamo la frase *to be willing*, volere (essere volonteroso o quando la volontà non è così assoluta i verbi *to wish*, *to desire*.

Volere innanzi un soggiuntivo italiano si rende con *will have* o *would have*, l'accusativo del soggetto e l'infinito senza il *to* del verbo che in italiano è al soggiuntivo, p. e.:

Vorrei che poneste maggior attenzione,   *I would have you pay more attention.*

I verbi difettivi non avendo participio passato non possono di conseguenza esser preceduti dall'ausiliare *to have* e però le frasi italiane *avrei dovuto, potuto, voluto* si traducono col condizionale dei verbi *will, shall, can, may, ought* a cui si fa seguire *to have* all'infinito senza il *to* e il participio passato del verbo principale.

Avrei voluto farlo,   *I would have done it*

Avreste potuto leggere più   *You could have read longer.*
a lungo,

to spare, risparmiare   *to be in a hurry*, aver fretta.

Dear Henry, I would have you come a little earlier. Shall I come at nine o'clock? Yes if you can. Will you repeat the english lesson now? No sir, I should like to repeat it to morrow. I would have you repeat it before breakfast. — Without a farthing in his pocket he will go to America. Will he? And why do you not counsel him for his good? He will not be counselled. He who will not listen to good advice cannot be helped. — Napoleon would have the whole world obey him, but the whole world would not have Napoleon for its master. — Shall I rise to morrow at six o'clock? No, I will not have you rise before eight o'clock as you are yet weak, and it might hurt you. My father will have me always speak english with my teacher. He is perfectly right. — Where are you going in such a hurry? I must go and call on my father in law who is dying. You should have gone earlier, now there is no time, the poor man is already dead. I would have gone this morning but it was quite impossible for me. Who could have thought of such a thing? You ought to have written me last week, if you had, such a misfortune could have been prevented. To spare them the mortification of a confession, they would have us say what was not true. Why are you in such a hurry? I would not have you put so many questions, if I am in a hurry, it is not your business.

327.

Perchè non avete condotto vostro fratello con voi? Egli avrebbe voluto venire a trovarvi ma fu impedito. Non voglio che gli diciate che ho chiesto di lui, se vuol venire a trovarmi tanto meglio, ma non voglio che egli creda ch'io non posso vivere senza vederlo; se egli mi amasse e avesse voluto che io creda al suo amore egli avrebbe dovuto scrivermi per scusarsi che non ha potuto venire. Siete troppo severo con lui, avreste dovuto vedere quanto egli era addolorato, e come non voleva mai che andassi, ma voleva che aspettassi per vedere se avesse potuto venire con me. — Avrebbe potuto essere un avvocato e invece è diventato un ciabattino. È peccato davvero. Io non lo compiango, nè voglio che lo compiangiate, egli non è degno di essere compianto. Non vorrei che parlaste sì malo dei vostri vecchi amici. Non avrebbe dovuto essere pigro e giuocatore, se non voleva che parlassimo male di lui. Ho fretta, addio, ritornerò dopo mezzogiorno. Perchè avete tanta fretta, non sono ancora le dieci? Devo andare alla ferrovia perchè non vorrei che un mio debitore scappasse.

328.

I verbi neutri o intransitivi, che sono quelli che non possono avere un oggetto diretto cioè a dire che l'azione resta in chi la fa, come *andare*, *venire*, si coniugano in inglese col verbo *avere* anzichè col verbo *essere* come in italiano p. e.:

Io son andato, *I have gone*.

Si possono però talvolta coniugarli col verbo *essere*, ma allora designano piuttosto uno stato che un'azione, p. e.:

Where is he? He is gone out.

I would have you go and see how is your teacher. I have already gone there, and they told me he is better. Do you know what has happened to him? He has fallen from his horse. Has he not a good horse? Yes, but he has run too fast. Why was he in such a hurry? Because they had told him that the king had arrived. You should have returned sooner, my dear boy, children ought not to remain out so late. I have remained out so late, because my uncle has kept me supping with him. But how did you hurt your hand? I have run to come as early as possible, because I was afraid you were uneasy about me, and I have fallen on the street. What do you long for? I long for my good friend, who has returned from America. Has he been long there? He has been there these three years. Whilst you were out the wholesale merchant came, he has brought an invoice which I have put on your table.

329.

Vorrei che mi diceste chi aspettate con ansietà? Aspetto con ansietà il signor Betti, mercante all' ingrosso, che è ritornato da Parigi e mi deve portare dei vestiti all'ultima moda. Che cosa vi è accaduto che siete tanto addolorato? Una gran disgrazia è accaduta ad un mio amico, gli hanno rubato dieci mila lire ed egli ha dovuto fallire. Vorrei che non vi addoloraste tanto per le disgrazie degli altri e che pensaste piuttosto al vostro povero padre che è andato alle Indie per far fortuna per voi; se non foste stato così pigro avreste potuto risparmiargli questa pena. Egli non vi è andato solo per me ma anche per i miei fratelli. Giovanni, è venuto il barbiere? Non ancora, signore. Andate a dirgli che lo aspetto perchè devo uscire. Subito signore. Eccolo che viene, ma non può farvi la barba perchè avendo corso per la strada egli è caduto e si è fatto male alla mano destra. Son due giorni che sono ritornato dalla campagna e ancora non vi ho veduto, venite alle quattro dopo mezzogiorno che dobbiamo metter in ordine i nostri conti.

330.

to get   *got*   *got*.

Questo verbo, secondo la frase in cui si trova, prende significati molto diversi. Ne daremo i significati più generali, dai quali mediante il buon senso e la pratica si potranno comprendere ed applicare gli altri.

Intanto osserveremo che esso è transitivo e intransitivo; come transitivo esso significa: *ottenere, raggiungere, cagionare, impegnare*, come intransitivo significa: *riuscire, arrivare, andare e diventare*, p. e :

He will get nothing by it, Non vi guadagnerà niente
I got very angry, Mi arrabbiai (diventai arrabbiato)
They got him to go home, Lo impegnarono ad andare a casa.

Indicheremo ancora alcune espressioni in cui codesto verbo prende alcune particolari significazioni, p. e.:

to get away, allontanarsi   *to get off*, scappare
» *asleep*, addormentarsi   » *into favour*, entrare in
» *by heart*, imparare a   favore
           memoria   » *ready*, approntarsi
» *down*, scendere   » *a suspicion*, concepir
                                   il sospetto
» *drunk*, ubbriacarsi   » *certain of*, accertarsi di

Ricorderemo inoltre che *got* participio passato di *to get*, è spessissimo pleonasmo, ciò succede quando unito al verbo *to have* esso indica il possesso, p. e.:

Have you got any money? Avete denaro?

for instance, per esempio   *fluctuating*, fluttuante
lately, ultimamente   *savings*, risparmi
the funds, i fondi   *to outwit*, vincere in astuzia
to employ, impiegare   *to add*, aggiungere.

I have lately got a considerable sum of money, please to advise me how to employ it. I should advise to employ it in public funds, for instance Italian rent. Public funds are now fluctuating I am afraid to employ my sum in them. —Get ready for half past six, we shall go and take a walk. I don't know if I am allowed to come as I have my German lesson to get by heart. — Add your savings to mine and let us get merchants, it is the only mean to get rich in a very short time. I have not got so great savings as you fancy and I would not wish to employ them in trade. Wouldn't you? Well, you will always remain a poor devil. I got a suspicion that the gentleman to whom I have trusted my savings is going to cheat me, how could I get certain of it in order to outwit him? It is very difficult, isn't? Tell him, for instance, you are going to employ your savings in a very good business, and that you mean to associate him to it, and to trust him all the savings you shall make I am told you have lately employed a great sum of money in public funds, I think you will repent, as public funds are always fluctuating. Try to get by heart these phrases and I'll add two francs to your savings.

331.

Mi si dice che il conte B. sia entrato nelle grazie del re, vorrei accertarmene, come devo fare? Non lo so davvero. Che cosa avete iu mano? Una lettera per il mio padrone. Perchè piangete? Perchè ho confidato i miei risparmi a un signore, e ho concepito il sospetto che voglia scappare e ingannarmi. Ditemi chi è, e procurerò di accertarmene. È il signor C. egli aveva impiegato tutto il suo denaro nei fondi, ed ora egli è diventato molto povero. Approntatevi per le sei e vi andremo assieme. Temo non ci guadagneremo nulla. Ma come avete voi confidato i vostri risparmi ad un uomo che non conoscevate? avreste dovuto piuttosto unirli a quelli di vostra sorella e impiegarli per esempio in commercio, a codesta maniera avreste potuto diventar ricche in breve tempo. Che cosa devo fare per imparare presto l'inglese? È vero che bisogna imparar molto a memoria? Non lo credo, procurate di avere buoni libri inglesi, per esempio le opere di Goldsmith, di Bulwer e leggeteli; in questa maniera riuscirete alla conoscenza della lingua inglese. M'addormento ogni volta che prendo un libro inglese in mano, ultimamente voleva leggere *Gli ultimi giorni di Pompei*, e m'addormentai alla seconda pagina.

332.

whereby, col mezzo di che
safe, salvo, sicuro
to appropriate, appropriarsi
to perceive, accorgersi
stock, capitale
clearsighted, di buona vista
safety { salvezza, sicurezza

THE CLEAR-SIGHTED BLIND MAN.

A blind man having got a considerable sum of money buried it in a little garden behind his house, where he used to visit it from time to time to assure himself of its safety, and to add his little savings. A neighbour having discovered the deposit, appropriated it to himself. The blind man soon perceived that his treasure had been stolen, and getting some suspicion that his neighbour was the thief, determined to get certain of it, and, if possible, to outwit him. He therefore got to his house and told him that he was come to get his advice on an important subject. Well, said the other, what is it? Why, « answered the blind man, » I have got a sum of money which I have hidden in a safe place, but so it lies a dead stock; now having lately got a legacy, I got in doubt, whether I had better bury it with the other, or place the whole in the public funds whereby I should get some interest. His neighbour advised him without hesitation not to risk his money in the funds, which were fluctuating and uncertain, but to deposit it as he had done the other in a secure place. As soon as the blind man got away, he (the neighbour) carefully replaced the money he had taken, thinking by that means to get both sums. The other, expecting that such would be the result, took his money, and shortly afterwards paid a visit to his *honest* neighbour to ask him which of the two he thought the most clearsighted.

Conversation.

Questions.	*Answers.*
What had a blind man got?	*He had got a considerable sum of money.*
Where did he bury it?	*He buried it in a little garden behind his house.*
What did he use to do there?	*He used to visit it from time to time.*
Why so?	*To assure himself of its safety, and to add his little savings.*
Did anybody discover it?	*Yes, a neighbour discovered it and appropriated it to himself.*
Did the blind man perceive that?	*Yes, he perceived soon that his treasure had been stolen.*
About whom did he get some suspicion?	*About his neighbour.*
What did he determine?	*He determined to get cer-*

	tain of it, and if possible to outwit him.
Where did he get then?	To his neighbour's.
What did he tell him?	He told him that he was come to get his advice on an important subject.
What was it?	He had got, said he, a sum of money hidden in a safe place.
About what was he in doubt?	Having lately got a legacy, he got in doubt, whether, etc.
Why would he place it in the public funds?	He would do so that he might get some interest.
What did his neighbour advise him to do?	His neighbour advised him without hesitation not to risk his money in the funds.
Why should he not?	Because the funds were fluctuating and uncertain.
Where did he advise him to deposit it then?	He advised him to deposit it as he had done the other, in a secure place.
What did the neighbour do afterwards?	As soon as the blind man got away, he carefully replaced the money he had taken.
What did he think in doing so?	He thought by that means to get both sums.
Which was the expectation of the other?	He expected that such would be result.
What did he do then?	He took his money and shortly afterwards paid a visit to his neighbour.
Did he ask him anything?	He asked him which of the two he thought the most clearsighted.

Ripetizione.

Quando si adopera in inglese il passato definito? E quando il passato indefinito o composto? Come si rende in inglese l'imperfetto italiano esprimente un'azione che è stata abituale? Come si traduce *è un'ora che, son due anni che?* Che cosa è *will* oltre che ausiliare? Come si traduce *vorrei che mi pagaste?* come, *avrei potuto andare?* Ditemi dei varî significati del verbo *to get got got.*

Lezione quarantesima terza. Lesson the forty third.

CONTINUAZIONE
DELLA SINTASSI E PARTICOLARITÀ DEL VERBO.

333.

Abbiamo già osservato nella prima parte che non tutti i verbi che sono riflessivi in Italiano lo sono pure in Inglese, molti già ne conosciamo, dei principali tra gli altri crediamo utile dar qui la nota:

Astenersi,	To abstain.	Correggersi,	To mend.
Svegliarsi,	,, awake.	Accorgersi,	,, perceive.
Prendersi cura,	,, care.	Impadronirsi,	,, seize.
Lamentarsi,	,, complain.	Rallegrarsi,	,, rejoice.
Battersi,	,, fight.	Ricordarsi,	,, remember.
Alzarsi,	,, get up, rise.	Pentirsi,	,, repent.
Ubriacarsi,	,, get drunk.	Ritirarsi,	,, retire.
Andarsene,	,, go away.	Sedersi, assidersi	,, sit down.
Affrettarsi,	,, hasten.	Arrendersi,	,, surrender.
Coricarsi,	,, lie down.	Ritirarsi,	,, withdraw.
Maritarsi,	,, marry.	Meravigliarsi,	,, wonder,
Imbarcarsi,	,, embark.	Prepararsi,	,, prepare.
Appoggiarsi,	,, lean.	Precipitarsi,	,, rush.

freshness, freschezza
the *complexion* { carnagione
colorito
cera
bettimes, per tempo
vessel, bastimento
to avert, stornare
habit, abitudine.

Charles the Tenth did not behave with the proper prudence in the French revolution of 1830, and when he was in Scotland. he remembered with regret, the happiness of former days. The French army has surrendered. It cannot be true, you are certainly mistaken.

Napoleon repaired to an English vessel when he was beaten at Waterloo. You are always complaining. I don't think you are really so unhappy as you say. No, we are indeed unhappy, yet, as we cannot avert our misfortune, we will submit to it like men. — Sit down Mr. Piacenti; how are you? Quite well. I rejoice to hear it, you must have risen betimes this morning. I awoke at five, I rose at half past five; but I went to bed early last night. It is, at least in part, to the early rising that you owe your robust health. Perhaps so. I wonder no more at the freshness of your complexion. — Did you hear that the ennemy has surrendered? — Lean on my arm my dear girl. If she had not leaned on the wall she would have fallen. Mend my dear boy, and every body will love you. I do nothing wrong, and I don't know what to do to mend. You are always quarelling, (*) and you wonder if I tell you to mend? Mend of your bad habits, if you care for your friend's love and esteem.

334.

Sedetevi, vi prego; come state? Dacché mi levo per tempo sto perfettamente bene. Me ne rallegro, infatti la vostra cera ha acquistato una freschezza che prima non aveva. Se siete stanco appoggiatevi al mio braccio. Non ho bisogno di appoggiarmi. Ho inteso che state per imbarcarvi su di un bastimento inglese che sta per partire per l'America, è vero? Si. Temo ve ne pentirete, vi prego, però, quando sarete nel nuovo mondo ricordatevi dei vecchi amici. Sicuramente mi ricorderò sempre di voi e della vostra bontà. Mi meraviglio che vostro padre che vi ama tanto vi permetta che vi imbarchiate per andarvene cosi lungi. Povero me, vi sentite male? Appoggiatevi al mio braccio. Non temete, non è nulla, mi hanno fatto ber tanto che quasi mi sono ubbriacato. Mi hanno detto che voi avete la cattiva abitudine di ubbriacarvi spesso.

(*) contendere.

— 94 —

335.

VERBI RECIPROCI.

to love each other, (o) one another.	Amarsi (l'un l'altro, li uni li altri).
We have always loved each other tenderly.	Ci siamo sempre amati teneramente.

In italiano i verbi riflessivi e reciproci sono nella forma plurale l'istessa cosa, p. o. *noi ci vediamo*, vuol dir tanto ognuno di noi vede sè stesso, come, ognuno di noi vede l'altro; in Inglese invece la bisogna corre altrimenti : nel primo caso si dirà *we see ourselves* (aggiungeremo per maggior schiarimento) *at the looking-glass*, (allo specchio) nel secondo caso si dirà *we see one another:* dunque i pronomi *ci, vi, si*, si tradurranno coi pronomi riflessivi *ourselves, yourselves, themselves*, quando chi fa e riceve l'azione è la medesima persona; si tradurranno invece coi reciproci *one another, each other*, quando di due o più persone ognuno riceve l'azione che l'altro fa.

to bequeathe, lasciar in eredità	*to value*, valutare
piteous, { lagrimevole / miserando	*shot*, tiro, sparo
	to despise, disprezzare.

Look at those two gentlemen, they have always been friends, they have a great stock in society, and should of course assist each other, instead of injuring and despising one another as they do. Do we not love one another tenderly? Yes that we do, and we shall always value and esteem each other. What has become of Mr. Vanni and Mr. Caico ? It is really a piteous story, they owed all to one another, and really esteemed and loved one another tenderly, unluckily they happened to fall in love with the same girl, they got angry, and after having challenged each other, they killed one another at the first shot. And what has become of the stock they had in society? They bequeathed it to the girl who caused their death. I am told they bequathed something also to you. Hear the shots, what is the matter? The Italian army is going into Rome.

336.

maledetto, *cursed* acerbamente, *harshly*
quando ci vedremo? *when shall we meet?*
ambizione, *ambition* progresso, *progress*.

Ci siamo sempre amati e stimati, il capitale che i nostri genitori ci hanno lasciato lo tenemmo in società per esser tutti e due o poveri o ricchi, ci siamo sempre assistiti nel bisogno, ed ora ci odiamo, ci disprezziamo e c'ingiuriamo, e ciò a causa del giuoco, maledetto il giuoco. È uno spettacolo miserando veder le nazioni odiarsi, distruggersi colla guerra per soddisfare all'ambizione di alcuni pochi, mentre che dovrebbero assistersi per avanzare insieme nella via del progresso. Giurerei che non vi amate più come altra volta, qualchecosa deve essere accaduto che vi fa dimenticare l'antica amicizia. Che cosa vi fa supporre ciò? Vedo che non vi parlate più con quella bontà con cui eravate abituati di parlarvi, e ciò che non m'accade mai prima, udii jer l'altro che vi siete ingiuriati acerbamente. — Quando ci vedremo per metter in ordine il nostro affare? Doman l'altro. — Badate di esser pronto al primo sparo. Non temete, io non ho l'abitudine di far aspettare la gente.

337.

Si adopera spesso il participio presente invece dell'infinito, dopo i seguenti verbi:

to *forbear*, }
to *help* } fare a meno
to *avoid* }
to *prevent*, impedire
to *defer* }
to *delay* } differire
to *put off* }

to *intend*, aver l'intenzione
to *cease*, cessare
to *continue*, continuare
to *finish*, finire
to *have done*, aver finito di
to *give up*, rinunciare
to *repent*, pentirsi
to *purpose*, proporsi.

Il participio presente preceduto dall'aggettivo possessivo o dal genitivo possessivo, sostituisce spesso anche il soggiuntivo, p. e.:

I am delighted at my friend's coming,	Godo moltissimo che venga il mio amico.
His letter was the cause of my not going,	La sua lettera fu causa che io non andassi.
to talk, (*) dire, ciarlare	*grown-up,* grande, cresciuto
security, garanzia	*to disobey,* dissobedire.

What do you intend doing to morrow? If I may prevent my father's seeing me, I intend reading Byron's Childe Harold. You should rather renounce reading that book than disobey your father. But he is wrong to forbid my reading it. If he dislikes your reading such books, it is your duty to obey. — I could not forbear embracing the sweet child, he is full of wit and intelligence. I am afraid you are mistaken, the child's being able to speak very much is no proof of his being able to think. You cannot give up opposing other people's words; I tell you, he is a very talented child, he reads and writes passably well, and I dare say if you knew him you could not help admiring him as other people do. Have you done talking nonseses? it may be as you say, but his being able to read and write is no great security for talent. Look at those five women, which of them look more infatuated? The eldest. Perfectly so, and I assure you I cannot help despising her. Do you? And why? Because a mother, who has four grown-up daughters, and two sons, should cease thinking of her beauty. — You don't believe my being able to study eight hours a day. I never questioned your being able, though I very much doubted your beeing

---

(*) Leggasi *tòk;* così pure in altri casi la combinazione *alk* si pronuncia egualmente, p. e.: *walk* che si legge *wòk;* la lettera *l* è anche muta nelle seguenti combinazioni *alf, 'alm, olk, ould.*

willing to do it. Have you done breakfasting? Not yet. Waiter, please to ask that gentleman if he has done reading the newspaper.

338.

Non posso far a meno di sprezzare coloro, che non cessano mai di parlar male degli altri, e non possono rinunciare a questa cattiva abitudine malgrado che conoscano che non possono a meno d'essere odiati da tutti. Non questiono se siate capace ma dubito che abbiate il tempo di farlo. — Quando avrete finito di leggere le opere di Milton compiacetevi di prestarmele. Non posso far a meno di ammirarvi, son cinque mesi che studiate l'inglese e già comprendete Milton. Dubitate forse che io lo comprenda? No davvero. Che cosa vi proponete di fare, se non vi paga ciò che vi deve? Se posso impedire che se ne vada lo farò arrestare. Non credo che riusciate a far ciò. Quando avrete finito di pranzare, scendete, ho qualcosa da dirvi. Se voi rinunciate a studiare il francese non riuscirete mai a trovare un buon impiego. Guardate vostro cugino quello è un giovane di talento, egli conosce parecchie lingue e guadagna dieci franchi al giorno. Non dubito che egli guadagni molto, ma il suo saper molte lingue non è alcuna garanzia di talento.

·339.

stabilire un giorno, *to appoint a day*
pungere, *to sting   stang   stung*
con cura e diligenza, *by care and industry*
esser corto a denari, *to be short of ready money*
prender in società, *to take into partnership*
defunto, *late, deceased*   vespa, *wasp*.

Compiacetevi di stabilire un giorno in cui ci possiamo veder per decidere come dobbiamo impiegare il capitale lasciatoci dal defunto nostro zio. Supponete forse che non avrete tempo sufficiente di sprecare ciò che quel buon uomo ha accumulato con cura e industria? Le vostre parole pungono come vespe, ma questa volta avete torto; egli è che son corto a denari e non so come fare a pagare i miei debiti. E come intendete impiegar quel denaro? Non lo so davvero. Se voi rinunciate al giuoco e vi proponete di lavorare, io vi prenderei in società, e lo spero che col capitale che ci fu lasciato, e continuando a lavorare con cura e diligenza in breve diventeremo ricchi, ma se continuate a far debiti .... Signore mi avete punto un' altra volta colle vostre parole, non mi piace entrare in società con chi mi punge ad ogni momento senza alcuna ragione. Non v' adirate se vi punsi è perchè vi amo. — Che cosa è accaduto, Maria? il sangue scorre dalla vostra mano. Non ve ne date pensiero mi sono punta con uno spillo, guardate. ha cessato di scorrere.

340.

the bustle, il trambusto, la briga
to be over, esser finito
recipe, ricetta

the remainder, il resto
neglect, trascuratezza
to conceal, nascondere

INGRATITUDE AND AVARICE PUNISHED.

A gentleman, who had acquired a considerable fortune by care and industry in trade, finding himself at an advanced age, became desirous of quitting the bustle of business, and of passing the remainder of his days in tranquillity. He had a son, newly married, whom he had taken into partnership, and he now gave up the whole business and stock to him. The son and his wife expressed their gratitude for his kindness, and assured him that their greatest attention should be to make him happy.

During some time, the old gentleman found himself very confortable with his son and daughter-in-law and hoped that his worldly cares were over. At length however he began to perceive a little inattention, which grew by degrees into absolute neglect. Stung by such base ingratitude, he communicated his affliction to one of his old friends, who consoled him by assuring him that he should soon receive the usual attention from his children, if he would follow his advice. "What would you have me do?" said the old gentleman. — "You must lend me 500 L. *(liv. ster.)*, and it must be done in presence of your son. — Five hundred pounds! I have not so many shilings at my disposal. — "Never mind," replied the friend, "I will furnish you, come with me." — He gave him the sum and appointed the following day for the experiment.

He called on him, in the morning about breakfasttime, and told him before his son and daughter, that he had an opportunity of making an excellent speculation, but was rather short of ready money. — "Dont't let that be an obstacle," said the old gentleman, "how much do you want?" — "About 500 L.," replied he. — "Oh! if that is all, it is at your service, and twice the sum if necessary." The old gentleman went to his desk, counted out the money, and told his friend to take his own time for payment. The son and his wife could but ill conceal their astonishment on finding, as they imagined, that their father had reserved a considerable sum of money, their conduct changed and from that day to his death the old gentleman had no reason to complain of want of attention.

He died some years after, having previously made is will, which he deposited in the hands of his old friend. It is the custom in England, on the day of funeral, to read the will of the deceased in presence of the family. It was opened and read; the son and daughter listened with great attention and hopeful anxiety. Judge what was their surprise on finding the only legacy, their father had bequeathed them, was a recipe how to reward ungrateful children.

Conversation.

How had a gentleman acquired a fortune?
What did he desire to do and to what purpose?
Whom had he taken into partnership?
What did he give up to his son?
How did the son and wife express their gratitude?
How did the old gentleman find himself now?
What did he hope?
But what did he perceive at length?
To whom did he communicate his affliction?
How did the friend console him, and what did he advise him to do?
Did the old man make any objection?
How did his friend remove the obstacle?
Which day did they appoint for the experiment?
At what time did the friend call on him?
What did he tell him?
What did the old man answer and do?
What was the consequence of the old man's trick?
What did he do previously to his death?
What custom exists in England about the reading of the will?
How did the son and daughter listen to it?
About what were they surprised?

Ripetizione.

Ditemi alcuni dei verbi riflessivi in italiano e che non lo sono in inglese? Ditemi i verbi che reggono il participio presente? Ditemi la differenza tra l'italiano e l'inglese nei verbi reciproci. Verbo irregolare *pungere*, *punsi*, *punto*.

Lezione quarantesima quarta.   Lesson the forty fourth.

SINTASSI E PARTICOLARITÀ DELL'AVVERBIO.

341.

Un gran numero di avverbi si forma aggiugendo la particella *ly* agli aggettivi. p. e.:

slow, lento   slowly, lentamente
warm, caldo   warmly, caldamente
pretty, bello, grazioso   prettily, graziosamente.

Molto regole vengono date dai grammatici intorno al posto dell'avverbio, ma perchè codeste regole sono pochissimo osservate nella pratica, ed anche dagli stessi grammatici sono accompagnate da un gran numero di eccezioni, crediamo più opportuno lasciar ciò alla pratica, tanto più che nella prima parte abbiamo già dati esempi abbastanza numerosi perchè lo studioso si sia formata un'idea abbastanza chiara dell'applicazione degli avverbi; noteremo soltanto:

1° Che gli avverbi che designano un tempo preciso si mettono o in principio o in fine della frase, p. e.:

Verrò domani { to morrow I shall come
              { I shall come to morrow

2° Che quando il verbo è attivo, non si può mettere l'avverbio tra il verbo e il suo oggetto, ma si metterà o prima del verbo o dopo l'oggetto, p. e.:

You spend your money im- Spendete imprudentemente
prudently.   il vostro denaro
This greatly alarmed the Ciò allarmò il re grande-
king   mente.

TABELLA DI AVVERBI NON ANCORA DATI.

first, dapprima
at once, { subitaneamente / alla volta
outside, { di fuori
without, { fuori
usually, usualmente
quickly, prestamente
aside, a parte
yonder, laggiù
elsewhere, altrove

suddenly, improvvisamente
inside, { dentro
within, { di dentro
consequently, conseguentemente
beforehand, { anticipatamente
in advance, {
straight on, { diritto
straight forward, {

the parcel, il pacchetto
thunder-bolt, fulmine
to amend, correggersi
to relapse, ricadere
step in, entrate

at a lower rate, a un prezzo più basso
repentance, pentimento
to undeceive, disingannare
customer, avventore.

Our young friend first appeared anxious to amend but he soon relapsed into his former state. We first supposed that his repentance was sincere, we were soon undeceived. Step in quickly, we must set off at once. Are we obliged to pay beforehand? If you have no objection, you are. The goods you have sent me are bad, my customers complain bitterly, make amend by sending me others, otherwise I shall be obliged to cease at once being your correspondent. You are perfectly right, the bad goods were sent you inadvertently, I shall soon make you the amend you ask me for; in the meantime, try to sell the parcel at a lower rate than usually. Go elsewhere and quickly, you are not allowed to remain here. We usually allow ourselves to be deceived by appearances. He is your junior, (*) it was he who first made use of im-

(*) più giovane, cadetto.

proper language, I consequently think that he owes you an apology. — Did you hear the thunder-bolt last evening? Yes, I was writing a letter at that time, and I took such a fright that I fell from my chair. I am sorry to hear your poor son, who was going better, has relapsed into his dangerous illness. — I have sent you the parcel of goods you have ordered, they are not of the first quality, therefore, I felt obliged to put them at a lower rate than usually.

342.

Entrate, partiremo presto, perchè dobbiamo essere domattina a Como. Se si deve pagare anticipatamente, non posso entrare perchè non ho denaro meco. Non importa pagherete domani quando saremo arrivati; quel pacchetto è pur vostro? Sì. Bene, presto datelo qui. — Ho ricevuto il pacco di merci che m'avete spedito, ma i miei avventori si lamentano che non sono della prima qualità, quindi bisogna che mi compensiate della perdita; dapprincipio sperava di poter vendere allo stesso prezzo ma tosto m'accorsi che doveva vendere a un prezzo più basso che al solito. — Perchè non mi riceveste jeri mattina quando venni a visitarvi? Vi prego caldamente di scusarmene, parlava allora di affari molto interessanti. Entrate, vi prego, ho una cattiva notizia da darvi, il vostro povero cugino è morto. Come, mi dissero jeri che stava meglio! È vero, ma poi ricadde e morì. Mi scuserete se inavvedutamente vi ho spedito merci cattive, vendetele tosto a quel prezzo che potete, e vi ricompenserò volentieri delle vostre perdite. Andiamo altrove, qui non c'è nulla da fare per noi.

343.

to see one home, accompagnare uno a casa
the Exchange, la Borsa   *corner*, angolo.

I have been yesterday afternoon at the teacher's you recommended me, with the intention to begin my english lessons; but he would have me pay beforehand, I have not yet begun, and am obliged to wait till the first of next month. Why is Mr. Barcia angry with you? When he left my uncle's house on tuesday evening, he would have me see him home, but he lives without the walls and I refused to go so far. You mistake my dear, he lives within the walls and not very far, from your uncle's house. Had I known this, I should certainly have accompanied him. I told you his repentance was not sincere, and that in no time he should have relapsed; now you are undeceived, I dare say. He took me aside and spoke me in the ear. Could you tell me the way to the Piazza della Signoria? Go straight on till the first corner, then turn to the left. Tell me, if you please, what is that palace yonder? It is the Exchange, sir.

344.

Di grazia di chi è quel bel palazzo laggiù. Esso è del signor Ricasoli. Davvero? Per dove si va al teatro Pagliano? Andate sempre diritto fino al terzo angolo, e poi voltate a destra. I nemici arrivarono improvvisamente e noi dovemmo darcela a gambe. Io avrei preferito morire piuttosto che scappare vergognosamente. Entrate di grazia, perchè volete restare di fuori? Fa molto freddo e potreste ricadere. Siate così gentile di accompagnarmi a casa, o almeno fino fuori delle mura, è così noioso far la strada soli. Vi accompagnerò volontieri, purchè camminiate più adagio del vostro solito. Farò come vi piace. Addio, non ho più tempo di chiacchierare, devo andare alla borsa. È lontana la borsa? No, vedete quel palazzo la giù, quella è la borsa.

345.

to sow, seminare   *sowed*   *sown*
reluctantly, con repugnanza   *in my room*, in mia vece

warehouse, magazzino   *at my own expense*, a mie
originally, originariamente   spese
broker, rigattiere   *to apply*, rivolgersi
proper, conveniente.

What a countryman is that broker? He is originally a native of France but he has been very long in England where he has a warehouse, he went there reluctantly, but he was forced by the misery of his family. He was originally a cobbler, and by care and industry he soon became a broker. What did you sow in your garden? Some vegetables, I had first sown also some flowers, but I had no time to take propre care of them, and I have ceased sowing any. He received reluctantly the parcel and brought it to the broker's warehouse. He must have learned at his own expense that only by acting with integrity one may be happy. As I am not perfectly well to day, I am obliged to send you my son in my room, you may settle our business with him. I do not feel obliged to make you any amend as I have sent you the parcel at my own expense. That is not acting with integrity, my dear, I shall reluctantly be obliged to apply elsewhere. I have learned at my own expense that I must trust to nobody and if you are not disposed to pay me beforehand, please to apply elsewhere. I beg your pardon, and am ready to make you proper amend, the bad goods you received were originally intended to somebody else, and they were inadvertently sent you.

346.

Non avrei mai creduto che poteste agir meco con sì poca integrità, se voi continuate così, se non mi risarcite subito della mia perdita, dovrò con ripugnanza rivolgermi altrove, e allora imparerete a vostre spese, che in commercio bisogna agire con maggior integrità. Mi duole che abbiate potuto pensare così male di me, fu inavvedutamente e non per ingannarvi che vi furon spedite quelle merci, le quali erano originariamente destinate ad un rigattiere della nostra città. Ve ne manderò delle altre in loro vece, oppure se potete venderle a un prezzo più basso, vi risarcirò della perdita come è mio dovere. — Che cosa state seminando? Delle viole. Non mi piacciono i fiori, io seminerei in loro vece dei legumi, anche perchè i fiori richieggono troppa cura. Anch'io sono della vostra opinione, e con ripugnanza seminai i fiori, ma mia moglie vuol avere un mazzetto tutte le mattine e non posso fare a meno di soddisfarla. Non mancate domani, dobbiamo andare al magazzino del rigattiere per scegliere le merci che ci abbisognano. Non temete, se anche io non potessi uscire manderò mio figlio in mia vece.

347.

From a Country Shopkeeper to a dealer in London, complaining of the badness of his goods.

Reading, June 8th, 18—.

SIR, — When I first began to correspond with you, it was my fixed resolution to act with integrity and honour, expecting the same conduct in return. I must confess that the goods you sent me for some time were as good as any I could purchase from another party, and so far I had no reason to complain. But the two last parcels sent are so bad, that I dare not offer them to my customers. Under these circumstances, I am reluctantly obliged to tell you, that unless you send me others in their room, I must either withdraw my correspondence, or shut my shop. Your immediate answer will oblige.

Yours, &c.

To——. (———)

The Answer to the preceding.

London, June 9th, 18—.

Sir,—I received yours, and am extremely sorry to hear the goods sent you were so bad. I know I had some such in my warehouse, but was determined to sacrifice them at a low rate, without ever thinking of their being sent to any of my customers, particularly so regular a correspondent as yourself. By some mistake my servants have inadvertently sent them, for which I am extremely sorry; but in order to make you amends, I send by the rail-way those which I had originally intended for you, at my own expense. I hope you will excuse this, and be assured you shall never be served in such a manner for the future.

I am, Sir,
Your humble servant,
To——.   (——).

348.

ricamo, *embroidery*	la brezza, *the breeze*
il porto, *the harbour*	risparmiare, *to save*
noleggiare, *to hire*	fare una girata in battello, *to*
la spiaggia, *the quay*	*row about*
gemere, *to groan*	riscatto, *ransom*
Dico, *I say* (*).	

A che cosa si applicano le vostre sorelle che le vedo lavorare giorno e notte? Lavorano di ricamo. Non guadagnerebbero abbastanza per vivere lavorando di giorno? Sì, ma devono risparmiare una gran somma di denaro per pagare il riscatto di un nostro zio che geme nella schiavitù da cinque anni. A quanto ammonta il suo riscatto? Cinquecento lire sterline. Ve le presterò io. Dav-

(*) È un intercalare molto usato, serve per chiamare l'attenzione di quelli a cui si parla; in qualche dialetto taliano l'abbiamo pure, come il *digo* del triestini.

vero? Ma come potrò io restituirvele? Non ve ne date pensiero, vi farò lavorare, e in meno di due anni mi avrete ricompensato della somma del riscatto che vi avrò pagato in anticipazione. Non so come fare a ringraziarvi della vostra bontà. — Vorreste essere così gentile da dirmi la via per il porto? Andate per di quà sempre diritto, alla fine della via volgete a sinistra. Grazie. A chi sono destinati questi libri? Originariamente erano destinati pel mio povero figlio, dopo la sua morte non so che farne. Andiamo a fare una girata in battello e godere questa gentil brezza. Volontieri. Dico, noleggiate questo battello? Sì signore. Quanto all'ora? Due scellini. Dico io, guardate che magnifico porto, e quanta gente passeggia sulla spiaggia. Il porto di Marsiglia è più bello di questo ma la spiaggia non mi piace, e non vi si gode una brezza così gentile. Usciamo, si fa tardi. — Dico, guardate che bei ricami, credete costeranno molto? Non lo so, entriamo nel magazzino e potremo domandare. Dico, come vendete questi ricami? Cinque scellini l'uno.

349.

seed, semente
fare, nolo
neatness, pulitezza
to concern, interessare
waterman, barcajuolo
the delivery, la consegna

journeyman { lavorante
             { giornaliero
to sail, veleggiare
to ply, adoprarsi, veleggiare,
  far il tragitto
to release, liberare
overseer, sopraintendente.

FILIAL LOVE AND MODEST BENEVOLENCE.

One Sunday evening, a young man, by name Robert, was sitting in his boat by the quay in the harbour of Marseilles, waiting for a fare. A person stepped in, but, observing the genteel appearance of the youth, and the neatness of his boat, was about to retire, thinking it was a pleasure-boat of some private person. Robert however called him, saying: Sir, my boat is for hire; where do you wish to go? — I only wish, replied the stranger, to sail about in the harbour to enjoy the freshness of the breeze of this fine evening, but I cannot believe you are a waterman. — Indeed I am not, said Robert, but on Sundays and other holidays I ply here with this boat because I am very anxious to save a sum of money. — What, said the gentleman, are the seeds of avarice already sown in your mind? — Alas! Sir, replied the humiliated Robert, did you know for what purpose I wish to save money, I am sure you would not blame me. — Well, perhaps I am mistaken; come, row me about the port, and tell me your story. They left the quay, and Robert thus commenced his little story: My father, Sir, now groans in slavery at Teutan; he was a broker here, and by his honest industry maintained his family in respectability. Unfortunately he embarked for Smyrna to superintend the delivery of a cargo in which he was concerned; the vessel was taken by a Barbary corsair, and my poor father must remain a slave till I can obtain a sum sufficient to pay his ransom, which the Barbarians have fixed to 2000 crowns, a sum that far surpasses our scanty means; however we do our best, and trust that Providence will second our exertions. My mother and sister work night and day at embroidery, I am a journeyman jeweller, and put by every sou, I possibly can, out of my wages. I intended to go over and offer myself as a slave instead of my father; but my mother supplicated me not to abandon her, fearing the Moors would keep us both; and besides that, she requests all the captains to refuse taking me on board. I have therefore no other means left but saving money as fast as I can, in order to acquire the stipulated sum. Such is my unfortunate story, Sir, and I think you will not now accuse me of avarice.

Pray, said the stranger, do you ever hear from your father? What is his name? — His master, replied the young man, is overseer of the palace-garden at Fez, and my father's name is Robert. As it began to grow dark, the passenger desired to land. As he stepped out of the boat, he put into Robert's hand a purse containing eight double lewis-d'or and ten crowns in silver.

About six weeks after this adventure, Robert, his mother and sister were taking their frugal supper of bread and fruit, talking of the generous stranger, and thinking how long it would be before they should be able to release the father, when suddenly the door opened, and, to their inexpressible surprise and joy, he himself entered into the apartment. After tenderly embracing his family, he inquired by what means they had been able to procure the money for his ransom in so short a time, as well as the sum which had been given him to supply his immediate wants, and to pay his passage to France.

They looked at each other with mutual astonishment; the father became alarmed, and, turning to Robert, said: Unfortunate boy, what have you done? Have I purchased my freedom at the expense of your integrity? Better had you left me in slavery to the end of my days. — Calm your apprehension, my dear father, said Robert, embracing him, I am not your deliver; but I think I know who is. He then related the story of the stranger, who had inquired with so much interest after the situation of his father, and declared he would never discontinue his search, till he would have discovered their generous benefactor.

One day he met him on the quay; he immediately approached him, calling him the guardian-angel of his family, and entreaten him to go and contemplate the happiness he had bestowed. The stranger appeared to follow the young man, but when they passed near the exchange, he disappeared in the crowd, and Robert could never afterwards find him. And never anybody would have discovered who it was, if after the death of *Montesquieu*, a bill of exchange had not been found among other papers, stating that 2500 crowns had been sent by him for the deliverance from slavery of a certain man named Robert.

Conversation.

Where was a young man named Robert sitting?
Who stepped into his boat?
Why was he about to retire?
What did Robert say to him?
What did the stranger say he wished?
What could he not believe?
How did Robert explain the circumstance?
What did the stranger accuse Robert of?
What did Robert reply?
What did the gentleman desire him to do?
How did Robert begin his relation?
What was his father?
Why had he embarked?
By whom was the vessel taken?
What ransom did the Barbarians fix for the father's deliverance?
What does the family do to get that sum?
What had Robert at first intended to do?
Why did his mother supplicate him not to abandon her?
What did she request the captains to do?
How did Robert conclude his story?
What question did the stranger ask him?
How did he answer?

Why did the passegger desire to land?
What did he put in Robert's hand as he went off?
What was the family doing six weeks after this adventure?
Who did suddenly enter?
What did the father inquire about?
How did they look at each other?
What were the father's feelings and what did he say to Robert?
How did Rober answer?
Whom did he meet one day?
How did he call him?
Did the stranger follow him?
But what did he do near the exchange?
Could Robert find him afterwards?
Who was he and how was it discovered?

Ripetizione.

Come si formano molti avverbi? Ditemi qualche regola intorno al posto di alcuni avverbi. Verbo irregolare, *seminare, seminai, seminato.*

Lezione quarantesima quinta. Lesson the forty fifth.

DELLE PREPOSIZIONI.

350.

Nel corso del nostro metodo abbiamo avuto occasione d'insegnar praticamente l'uso delle preposizioni; considerata però la grande importanza ch'esso hanno nella lingua inglese e come il loro uso spessissimo sia diverso dall'italiano, abbiamo creduto opportuno di dedicarvi due lezioni.

La preposizione *di* si traduce (oltre le maniere che conosciamo) per *with* quando precede l'espressione che indica il mezzo onde l'azione espressa dal verbo ha avuto luogo, p. e.:

He was wounded with a sword (sōrd), fu ferito di spada
To tremble with cold, tremar di freddo.

Dopo gli aggettivi si traduce tanto con *of* che con *with* e *to*; dopo i participi passati si traduce con *with*, p. e.:

I am tired with walking
The trees are loaded with fruits, gli alberi sono carichi di frutta.
I am happy to see you in good health.

Spesso si traduce con *by*, p. e.:

by day, by night, di giorno, di notte
I know him by name, lo conosco di nome
by sight, di vista
he profits by his talents, approfitta dei suoi talenti.

La preposizione *a* si traduce qualche volta con *by, at*, p. e.:

to sell at auction, vendere all'incanto
by retail, al minuto.

Qualche volta per *on*, p. e.:
on horseback, a cavallo   *on foot*, a piedi
I did not do it on purpose, non lo feci a posta.

It is my turn, tocca a me   *It is your turn*, tocca a voi
to deal, fare   far male,
weapon, arme   *to ail* { soffrire
what ails you? di che soffrite?
I have a sore-throat, ho il mal di gola.

Whose turn is it to deal the cards? It is Mr. Vannuci's turn. I beg your pardon he has dealt them just now; it is my turn. Each in his turn. What ails you? You are very pale. I am tired with walking. Dear me, you came on foot, such a long way; for my part I came on horseback. If I had a horse I should also have come on horseback. Take care you have soiled my coat. Don't be angry I did not do it on purpose. You'll spoil your eyes if you work so much by night. I must work by night because I have no time to work by day. Please to introduce me to that gentleman, I am very desirous to make his acquaintance. I am sorry, I am not acquainted with him, I know him only by name and I know he is a talented gentleman who profits by his talents. Don't get asleep my dear, it is your turn now. About what are they chatting? About that wicked young man, who will never put his hand to any work. He is an ill bred fellow, he sleeps by day and amuses himself by night. Dear me you have wounded my hand. I did not do it on purpose. But you ought not to carry weapons about. I met yesterday your fair sister at the Earl's house, I would have her sing something, but she refused to comply with my request, she said, she had a sore-throat.

351.

Di chi è quell'arme che tenete in mano? Essa è di quel signore che parlava or ora meco, egli me l'ha data per farla raccomodare. Lo conoscete? Lo conosco di vista ma non lo conosco di nome. Vorreste essergli presentato? Vorrei. Veniste in carrozza o a cavallo? Venni a piedi. Davvero? Dovete essere stanco dal camminare, sedete. Sono abituato a camminare, quand' era più giovane camminava cinque o sei ore al giorno. Guardate quegli alberi come son carichi di frutta. Ma voi tremate. Sì, tremo di freddo. Di che soffre il povero Giorgio che è sì pallido? Son due settimane che ha il mal di gola. Dove si vendono questi libri? All' Incanto. Li vendono anche al minuto? Sì, potete prenderne quanti vi fa piacere. È vero che all' incanto vendono anche armi? Non ne ho vedute. Date qui, tocca a me a fare le carte. No signore, tocca alla signora. V' ingannate io le ho fatte adesso. Allora tocca a me. Badate m' avete dato due carte di meno. Scusate non l'ho fatto apposta. Ha versato l'inchiostro sui miei pantaloni e me li ha sciupati. Non andate in collera non l' ha fatto a posta. Di che soffrite? Ho il mal di gola. Studiate troppo di notte. Non credo che ciò mi faccia avere il mal di gola.

352.

La preposizione *da* si traduce generalmente con *from* quando implica un'idea di distacco, di partenza, o con *by* quando esprime l'agente.

Inoltre abbiamo alcune frasi in cui la preposizione *da* si traduce in modi peculiari, p. e.:

He spoke to me like a friend, mi parlò da amico
It is a subject worthy of you, è questione da voi
Matters of little weight, cose da poco
House to let, to ell, casa da affittare, da vendere
This way, that way, da questa parte, da quella.

Per col verbo *passare* o *andare* si traduce con *by* e *through*, p. e.:

I went to Naples by sea, andai a Napoli per mare
The rail-way passes through Foggia, la strada ferrata passa per Foggia.

Notiamo le seguenti frasi:

As you value life, per quanto vi è cara la vita
by the post, per la posta
All's over with him, è finita per lui
As for me I would not do it, per me non lo farei.

Con quando esprime il mezzo dell'azione si traduce con *by*, p. e.:

He enriched himself by robbing, si arricchì col rubare

$$\text{Fra} \begin{cases} between \\ among \end{cases}$$

Between hope and fear, fra il timore e la speranza
Among the poor, fra i poveri

to get into a passion, andar in collera
to have a competency, aver di che vivere; *hill* collina.

When do you intend going to London, and which way will you take? I am going next week, I shall go by Hamburg. I should think better to go through France by Calais. Where do you come from? I come from Spain, I have passed through the Pyrenees. All is over with me. Why then? I can't tell it you. Between friends there should be no secret. I don't see any friend here, I'm among enemies. As you value life do not get into a passion for matters of little weight. Do you call matters of little weight, my honour, my happiness? Pray do listen to me, I speak to you like a friend; you are in the wrong way, if you go on thus, all is really over with you. — By assiduous and well directed industry every one is sure to gain a competency. And many a man who had a competency lost it by his sloth and negligence. The rail-road between Milan and Venice passes through a tunnel under the hill of Vicenza. What is become of Mr. Piacenti? Poor devil, all is over with him, he is deep fallen in love, and between hope and fear he is dying. I am sorry indeed, as for me a girl could never make me unhappy. As you value life, follow my advice, otherwise you will bitterly repent. They are matters of little weight, my dear; I have a competency, and I don't care about any thing else.

353.

Per quanto vi è caro l'onore, ascoltatemi, vi parlo da amico, non fate affari con quell'uomo, egli si arricchì col rubare, e l'affare che vi propone non ò da voi. Non so come fare per dirglielo. Scrivetegli una lettera per la posta. Quando partite? Il quindici del mese prossimo. Andrete per mare o colla ferrovia? Non so ancora. Sapete se la ferrovia passa per Foggia? Credo di sì. — Come sta il figlio del sig. Nelli? Ho inteso che c'era poca speranza di salvarlo. Sono sempre fra il timore e la speranza; povero signore, se egli perde quel ragazzo la è finita per lui. Egli mi parlò da amico e non lo volli ascoltare, adesso me ne pento amaramente, ma non è più tempo, ora la è finita per me. Non ve ne date pensiero, son cose da poco, per me gli scriverei e tenterei di farlo ritornare; in ogni modo egli è tra amici e sono sicuro non manca di nulla.

354.

In dopo un verbo di moto si traduce per to o into, p. e.:

She is gone to England, è andata in Inghilterra
Let us go into the coffee-house, andiamo in caffè
within eight days, in otto giorni
In a fortnight, in quindici giorni
at all events, in ogni caso
above, al di sopra, sopra
below | al di sotto
beneath
beyond, oltre

within, dentro
without, fuori
nay, anzi
as far as, fino (delle distanze)

beside, accanto   *but for*, senza, se non fosse
besides, in oltre, di più
but for the bad weather, senza il cattivo tempo — se non fosse il cattivo tempo.

to seek, cercare   *sought*   *sought*
to seek after, informarsi   *the story*, il piano
to urge, sollecitare   *the path*, il sentiero
close, vicinissimo, accanto, rasente.

It is not beneath the dignity of a nobleman to be a merchant, in England there are plenty of merchants among the noblemen. Within an hour I shall be here again. I believe my money has fallen into bad hands. The child went alone into the garden and fell into the well. Seek the book. I sought it, but couldn't find it. I took a walk without the walls, and I am very tired of walking. But for the bad weather I should have gone farther, and sought after my poor teacher, who lives without the walls. But for you I should have urged him to go in. At all events he will return. I hope. Yes, he will return within eight days. He was beside me, I urged him to get on, but he stood unmoved, nay he was willing to go back. But for his tender age I should have beaten him. Does he live in the same house with you? Yes, in the story above mine. And Mr. Bonetti? In the story below. But for the rain I would accompany you as far as Cavour-street. He urged me to accept his invitation but I declined it. Why did you decline it? Because he lives without the walls; besides he is a very tiresome fellow. What are you seeking? I am seeking the right way to that church yonder. I think by this path the way is shorter. Beyond that church, close to the garden, there is the church-yard. What have you sought in that basket? I sought a pen, which I want. Have you been long at Paris? Only a fortnight.

355.

Senza il suo aiuto io non avrei mai ottenuto quel posto, anzi se non fosse lui che mi sollecitò ad accettarlo io avrei declinato un tal onore, ed ora me ne pentirei amaramente; inoltre fu lui che mi fu sempre accanto ogni qual volta ebbi bisogno di un buon consiglio e di aiuto, come potrei essere ingrato? Potreste dirmi ove egli dimora? Fuori delle mura, alla casa in cui dimoro io, nel piano disopra a quello del medico. Mi sollecitò ad entrare nel giardino. Io non avrei declinato l'invito, se non fosse per il timore che i miei figli che, come sapete, sono molto fieri, potessero cadere nel pozzo. Credete che arriverà entro quindici giorni? Credo che arriverà prima, anzi ho inteso, che è già partito da Londra. Fin dove ha egli viaggiato? Fino nella Norvegia. Vi siete informato del sentiero più breve per arrivare dal medico? Me ne sono informato e mi ha detto che è quello accanto alla chiesa, io l'ho cercato ma non l'ho potuto trovare. Mi scrisse che avrebbe saldato il nostro conto in otto giorni; ora son già passati quindici giorni e non ha mantenuta la parola.

356.

egoista, *selfish*
dimora, *abode*
aver simpatia, *to have a liking*
daddovero
proprio sul serio } *in right earnest*
desiderare con ardore, *to covet*
traccia, *track*
dar vita, *to enliven*
dar occhiate attorno, *to glance about*
ci condusse fuor di strada, *led us astray*.

Venite, vi si desidera ardentemente, sapete bene che voi date vita alla nostra società, siete un egoista di venire così tardi; m'immagino che sarete venuto a piedi. Siete troppo buono; ma sapete che non posso sopportare di andare a cavallo, pure sarei arrivato prima, senza una falsa traccia che mi condusse fuori di strada. Vorreste presentarmi a quella signorina che siede accanto a vostra cognata? Mi rincresce, non la conosco che di nome, non le ho mai parlato, ma perchè vorreste esserle presentato? Vi parlerò da amico, ho una gran simpatia per quella ragazza. Davvero? Parlate proprio sul serio? Sicuramente; guardate, essa dà attorno delle occhiate, credete cerchi qualcuno? Sì, il suo amante. Povero me essa ha un amante! Allora la è finita per me. Siete un egoista. Un uomo che avevamo pregato di indicarci la via, ci condusse fuori di strada per rubarci, ci condusse nella dimora di un contadino, ma vostro cognato avendo dato alcune occhiate all'intorno entrò in sospetto; senza di lui, ci avrebbero probabilmente rubato e forse uccisi. Vi prego di non scherzare. Io non ischerzo, io parlo proprio sul serio. Tanto peggio allora. Cosa volete dire? In quindici giorni lo saprete.

357.

loft, soffitta	*gently*, adagino
dreadful, terribile	*charcoal burner*, carbonajo
benighted, sorpreso dalla notte	*cutlass*, coltellaccio
to beseech, pregare	*to omit*, ommettere
mistress, amante	*to prate*, cianciare
ladder, scala a piuoli	*to creep*, arrampicarsi
to breath, respirare	*wicked*, malvagio, cattivo.

A DREADFUL ADVENTURE.

I was one day travelling in Calabria (says Courier in a letter to his female cousin.) It is a country of wicked people, who, I believe, have no great liking to any body, and are particularly ill-disposed towards the French. To tell why would be a long affair. It is enough that they hate us to death, and that the unhappy being, who should chance to fall into their hands, would not pass his time in the most agreeable manner. I had for my companion a fine young fellow. I do not say this to interest you — but because it is the truth. In these mountains the roads are precipices, and our horses got on with the greatest difficulty. My comrade going first, a track, which appeared to him more practicable and shorter than the regular path, led us astray. It was my fault. Ought I to have trusted to a head of twenty? We sought our way out of the wood, while it was yet light; but, the more we looked for the path, the farther we were off it. It was a very black night, when we came close upon a very black house. We went in, and not without suspicion, But what was to be done? There we found a whole family of charcoal burners at table. At the first word they invited us to join them. My young man did not stop for much ceremony. In a minute or two we were eating and drinking in right earnest — he at least: — for my own part I could not help glancing about at the place and the people. Our hosts indeed looked like charcoal burners; — but the house! — you would have taken it for an arsenal. There was nothing to be seen but muskets, pistols, sabres, knives, cutlasses. Every thing displeased me, and I saw that I was in no favour myself. My comrade, on the contrary, was soon one of the family. He laughed, he chatted with them; and with an imprudence, which I ought to have prevented, he at once said where we came from, where we were going, that we were Frenchmen. Think of our situation. Here we were amongst our mortal enemies, alone, benighted, far from all human aid. That nothing might be omitted that could tend to destroy us, he must play the rich man, promising these folks to pay them well for their hospitality; and then he must prate about his port-manteau, earnestly beseeching them to take great care of it and put it at the head of his bed, for he wanted no other pillow. Ah, youth, youth, how you are to be pitied ! Cousin, they might have thought we carried the diamonds of the crown : the treasure in his port-manteau, which gave him such anxiety, consisted of the letters of his mistress.

Supper ended, they left us. Our hosts slept below; we on the story where we have been eating. In a sort of hanging loft, seven or eight feet high, where we were to mount by a ladder, was the bed that awaited us — a nest into which we had to introduce ourselves by creeping under beams, loaded with provisions for all the year. My comrade seized upon the bed above, and was soon fast asleep with his head upon the precious portmanteau. I was determined to keep awake, so I made good fire, and sat down. The night was almost passed over tranquilly enough, and I was beginning to be comfortable, when just at the time when it appeared to me that day was about to break, I heard our host and his wife talking and disputing bellow me; and putting my ear into the chimney, which communicated with the lower room, I perfectly distinguished these exact words of the husband: — *Well, well, let us see,— shall we kill them both?* To which the wife replied: *Yes,* — and I heard no more.

How shall I tell you the rest? I could scarcely breathe; my whole body was as cold as marble; to have seen me, you could not have told whether I was dead or alive. Heavens! when I yet think upon it. We two were almost without arms; against us were twelve of fifteen men who had plenty of weapons. And then my comrade dead of sleep and fatigue! To call him up, to make a noise, was more than I durst; to escape alone was an impossibility. The window was not very high, but under it were two great dogs, howling like wolves, Imagine if you can the distress I was in. At the end of a quarter of an hour, which seemed an age, I heard some one on the staircase, and through the chink of the door I saw the old man, with a lamp in one hand and one of his knives in the other. He mounted, his wife after him; I was behind the door. He opened it; but, before he came in, he put down the lamp, which his wife took up, and coming in, with his feet naked, she being behind him, said in a smothered voice, hiding the light partially with her fingers: *Gently, go gently.* When he reached the ladder, he mounted, his knife between his teeth; and going to the bed where that poor young man lay with his throat uncovered, with one hand he took his knife, and with the other — ah, my cousin — he seized a ham which hung from the ceiling, cut a slice, and retired as he had come in. The door is shut up again, the light vanishes, and I am left alone to my reflections.

When the day appeared, all the family with a great noise came to rouse us, as we had desired. They brought us plenty to eat, they served us a very proper breakfast I assure you. There were two capons, of which, said the hostess, you must eat one and carry away the other. When I saw the capons, I at once understood the meaning of those terrible words — *Must we kill them both!*

Conversation.

To whom was Courier writing a letter?
Where did he say he was travelling?
What was his opinion about the Calabrian people?
Towards whom are they particularly ill-disposed?
Who was Courier's companion?
What sort of roads are there in Calabria?
How did the horses get on?
What led the travellers astray?
Whose fault was it?
Did they not seek their way out of the wood?
To what sort of a house did they come?

Did they go into it?
Whom did they find there?
To what did these people invite them?
Did the travellers accept?
What did Courier observe while glancing about?
What did his companion do on the contrary?
Where did he say they came from?
What did he prate about?
What could the people suppose the port-manteau to contain?
What did it really contain?
In which room were the travellers to sleep?
Where was their bed and how were they obliged to introduce themselves into it?
How did the night pass?
What did Courier hear just about day-break?
What did he hear the husband asked his wife?
What was the wife's answer?
How had he heard that?
What was Courier's sensation in this moment?
What did he hear on the staircase?
What did he see through the chink of the door?
What did the old man do before he came in?
How did he enter?
Whose bed did the man approach?
What did he take with one hand?
What did he seize and do?
When and how did the family rouse the travellers?
How was breakfast, and what was served up?
What did the hostess say to them?
What did they understand now?

Ripetizione.

Ditemi le diverse maniere di tradurre le preposizioni *di, a, da, per, in, con,* verbo irregolare *cercare, cercai, cercato.*

Lezione quarantesima sesta. Lesson the forty sixth.

DELLE PREPOSIZIONI

che accompagnano i verbi modificandone il senso.

358.

La modificazione prodotta nel senso del verbo dalla preposizione che vi è unita, spesso non consiste in altro che nell'aggiungere al significato del verbo quello della preposizione, p. e.:

$$to\ go \begin{cases} in, & \text{entrare} \\ out, & \text{uscire} \\ up, & \text{salire} \\ down, & \text{discendere} \\ away, & \text{partire.} \end{cases}$$

Spessissimo però accade che la preposizione modifica il senso del verbo, cosicchè il significato che ne risulta è tale che non si spiega direttamente dal significato primitivo del verbo e della preposizione, p. e.:

to call, chiamare   to call on, far visita.

Di questi verbi crediamo necessario di dare una lista, perchè troppo importante è il loro uso nella lingua inglese.

LISTA DE' VERBI SEGUITI DA PREPOSIZIONI. (*)

VERBI.	PREPOS.	ESEMPJ.
To abide *Dimorare.*	by.	I abide by my determination. *Mantengo saldo il mio proposito.*
To acquaint *Avvertire.*	with.	I got acquainted with him at Mrs. C's. *Io feci conoscenza con lui in casa della signora C.*
To account *Spiegare,*	for.	I cannot account for it. *Non saprei dar ragione di questo.*

(*) In parte dal *Millhouse.*

VERBI	PREPOS.	ESEMPJ.
To act	up to.	He acts up to his principles.
Agire.		Agisce secondo i suoi principj.
To aim	at.	I aim at it.
Mirare.		Prendo questo di mira.
To alight	from.	He alights from his horse.
Smontare.		Smonta dal suo cavallo.
To answer	for.	I answer for it.
Rispondere.		Lo guarentisco.
To apply	to.	I apply to you for that.
Applicare.		M'indirizzo a voi per questo.
To atone	for.	Has he atoned for his temerity?
Espiare.		Ha egli scontato la sua temerità?
To attain	to.	You will never attain to it.
Pervenire.		Non vi giungerete mai.
To awe	into.	He awed him into silence.
Far stare a segno.		Lo fece tacere, lo tenne in timore.
To bargain	for.	I have bargained for a horse.
Patteggiare		Ho pattuito (per) un cavallo.
To beat	back.	We beat back the enemy.
Battere.		Noi respingemmo il nemico.
——	up.	We beat up their quarters.
		Attaccammo i loro quartieri.
To beg	for.	He begged for mercy.
Mendicare, chiedere.		Chiese pietà.
——	of.	I beg of you to forgive him.
		Vi prego di perdonarlo.
To bind	up.	The surgeon bound up his wounds.
Legare.		Il chirurgo fasciò, medicò le sue piaghe.
To blot	out.	His name is blotted out.
Imbrattare coll'inchiostro.		Il suo nome è scancellato.
To blow	out.	Blow out the candel.
Soffiare.		Spegnete la candela.
		He blew out his brains.
		Si fece saltar le cervella.
——	up.	They blew up the powder magazine.
		Hanno fatto saltare in aria la polveriera.
——	down.	That house has been blown down.
		Il vento ha mandato a terra quella casa.
To board	at.	I board at Mr. Bull's.
Stare a dozzina.		Sto a dozzina dal sig. Bull.
To break	down.	They have broken down the hedge.
Rompere.		Hanno abbattuto la siepe.
——	forth.	The sun breaks forth (throug the clouds).
	through.	Il sole dissipa le nuvole.
——	off.	He broke off the negociation.
		Egli troncò la negoziazione.

VERBI	PREPOS.	ESEMPJ.
To bring *Recare.*	about.	You can never bring it about. *Non potrete mai effettuarlo, venirne a capo.*
— —	forth.	The Queen has brought forth a prince. *La Regina si è sgravata d'un principe.*
—	over.	Leaving India he brought over (the sea) L. 30,000. *Ritornando dalle Indie recò seco L. 30,000.*
To brood *Covare.*	over.	He broods over his misfortunes. *Non fa altro che pensare alle sue disgrazie.*
To brush *Spazzolare.*	by.	He brushed by me in the crowd. *Egli mi passò bruscamente nella folla.*
To burn *Bruciare.*	out.	The fire is burnt out. *Il fuoco è spento.*
To burst *Crepare.*	into.	She burst into tears. *Ella si sciolse in lacrime.*
To call *Chiamare.*	on.	I will call on you at six. *Verrò a casa vostra alle sei.*
To carry *Portare.*	on.	They carry on the war. (*) *Si continua la guerra.*
To cast *Gettare.*	down.	He is quite cast down. *È molto afflitto, abbattuto, avvilito.*
— —	up.	Have you cast up my account? *Avete fatto il mio conto?*
To clear *Chiarire.*	up.	The weather clears up. *Il tempo si rasserena, si schiarisce.*
To come *Venire.*	by.	How did you come by it? *In che modo l'avete avuto?*
To confide *Confidare.*	in.	Do not confide in him. *Non vi fidate di lui.*
To comply *Condiscendere.*	with.	He complies with my request. *Condiscende alla mia domanda.*
To correspond *Corrispondere.*	with.	I correspond with my cousin Bull. *Carteggio col mio cugino Bull.*
To deal *Negoziare.*	with.	You have dealt nobly with me. *M'avete trattato molto bene.*
To depend *Dipendere.*	on.	That depends on you. *Ciò dipende da voi.*
To die *Morire.*	away.	The music dies away. *La musica cessa a poco a poco.*
To dine *Pranzare.*	upon.	We dined upon roast beef. *Mangiammo manzo arrosto a pranzo.*
To dispose *Disporre.*	of.	He had disposed of his house. *Aveva venduta la sua casa.*

(*) *On accenna quasi sempre la continuazione dell'azione espressa dal verbo che lo precede.*

VERBI.	PREPOS.	ESEMPJ.
To dream Sognare.	away.	In this solitude would I dream away the rest of my days. *In questa solitudine vorrei passare fantasticando il resto de' miei giorni.*
To dwell Dimorare.	upon.	I will not dwell upon that subject. *Non voglio ragionare distesamente sopra questo soggetto.*
To do Fare.	away. with.	That difficulty is done away with. *Quella difficoltà è tolta.*
To dote Vaneggiare.	on.	He dotes on her. *Egli l'ama soverchiamente, perdutamente.*
To fall Cadere	upon.	The wolves fell upon the sheep. *I lupi si avventarono su le pecore.*
——	in.	I fell in with an old friend. *Mi abbattei a caso in un vecchio amico.*
To fire Sparare.	at.	I fired at him. *Gli feci uno sparo addosso.*
To find. Trovare.	out.	I have found out the secret. *Ho scoperto il secreto.*
To gaze Mirare.	on, at.	Why do you gaze on it so? *Perchè lo mirate fisso fisso?*
To give Dare.	up.	I give up all pretension, all hope. *Abbandono ogni pretensione, speranza.*
——	in.	He will not give in, over. *Non vuol cedere, darsi per vinto.*
——	over.	The doctors have given him over. *I medici lo hanno abbandonato.*
To go Andare.	off, away.	I am going off, away. *Me ne vado.*
——	on.	Go on, (read on.) *Andate pure, (seguitate a leggere.)*
——	over.	He went over to the enemy. *Egli passò dal nemico.*
To happen Accadere.	upon.	I happened upon it. *Lo trovai a caso.*
To hear Udire.	out, through.	Hear me out (through) before you judge. *Prima di giudicare ascoltatemi sino alla fine.*
To help. Ajutare.	up.	Help him up. *Aiutatelo ad alzarsi, a montare, ecc.*
——	on.	I help him on. *Lo faccio avanzare.*
——	to.	Shall I help you to some pease? *Vi servirò dei piselli.*
To hit Colpire.	on.	You have hit the nail on the head. *Avete indovinato, dato nel segno.*
To hold Tenere.	out.	He held out his hand, a reward, etc. *Egli stese la mano, offrì una ricompensa, ecc.*

VERBI.	PREPOS.	ESEMPJ.
To impose *Imporre.*	upon.	I fear to be imposed upon, taken in. *Temo di essere ingannato, truffato.*
To keep *Custode.*	up.	Keep up your state. *Mantenete il vostro fasto.*
To knit	together.	A family knit together in the bonds of the tenderest affection.
Far lavori di maglie.		*Una famiglia congiunta in vincoli dell'affetto più tenero.*
—	up.	He knit up his brows. *Increspò la fronte, aggrottò le ciglia.*
To knock *Percuotere.*	down.	I knocked him down with my fist. *Lo atterrai col pugno.*
—	off.	He has knocked off his chains. *Ha rotto le sue catene.*
To laugh *Ridere.*	at.	What are you laughing at? *Di che ridete?*
—	—	You will be laughed at. *Sarete deriso.*
To lay	in.	We have laid in our provision of wood for the winter.
Porre.		*Ci siamo provveduti di legna per l'inverno.*
—	out.	You lay out too much money. *Spendete troppo denaro.*
—	hold of.	Lay hold of that plank. *Afferrate quella tavola.*
—	by.	He lays by (up) all he makes. *Pone in serbo tutto ciò che guadagna.*
—	waste.	They laid waste the country. *Diedero il guasto al paese.*
—	—	I will lay you fifty pounds. *Scommetto con voi cinquanta lire sterline.*
To leave *Lasciare.*	off.	We left off at page the fortieth. *Siamo rimasti a pagina quaranta.*
To let *Lasciare, permettere.*	loose.	Let loose the dogs. *Sguinzagliate i cani.*
—	in, out.	Let him in, out, etc. *Permettetegli di entrare, uscire, ecc.*
—	out.	He lets out horses. *Dà cavalli a nolo.*
To light *Accendere.*	upon.	I lit upon it in the street. *Lo trovai per caso nella strada.*
To lock *Serrare.*	up.	He has locked up the box. *Ha chiuso la cassetta con la chiave.*
—	out.	He locked me out last night. *Mi chiuse fuori della porta la notte scorsa.*
To look *Guardare.*	at.	Look at that spider. *Guardate quel ragno.*

— 130 —

VERBI.	PREPOS.	ESEMPI.
—	out for.	I am looking out for a wife. Cerco una moglie.
—	out of.	She is looking out of the window. Guarda dalla finestra.
—	upon.	I look upon it as a great honor. Lo stimo un grand'onore.
—	in.	I will look in ten minutes this evening. Questa sera verrò da lei per fermarmi 10 minuti.
To make Fare.	over.	I will make over my properly to you. Vi rimetterò la mia sostanza.
—	out.	He is making out the account. Sta facendo il conto.
—	up.	I shall soon make up my losses. Tosto riparerò le mie perdite.
—	out.	I can't make out the meaning of it. Non ne posso capire il senso.
—	up.	I made up to him. M'incamminai verso di lui.
—	way.	Make way. Fate piazza, fate largo.
To meet Incontrare.	with.	He has met with an accident. Gli è sopraggiunto un accidente.
To mutter Borbottare.	out.	He mutters out some words. Borbotta qualche parola.
To pack Imballare.	off.	He packed off last night. Se ne andò (di nascosto) la notte scorsa.
To part Separare.	with.	I cannot part with her (him, it, etc.) Non posso dividermi, separarmi da lei.
To pass Passare.	over, on.	I passed over on the ice. Ho passato il fiume sul ghiaccio.
To pay Pagare.	for.	I pay for my house. Pago la mia casa.
To peep. Far capolino.	at.	She is peeping at us through the persian. Ella ci guarda (di segreto) per la persiana.
To pine. Languire.	for.	He pines for liberty. Sospira la libertà.
To pique Vantarsi.	one's-self upon.	He piques himself upon his dancing. Si picca, si vanta del suo ballare.
To play Divertirsi.	on.	He plays on the violin. Suona il violino.
To point Additare.	at.	He is pointing at you. Vi mostra a dito.
—	out.	He pointed him out to me. Me lo additò, me lo indicò col dito.
To pore Fissar la vista.	over.	I found him poring over an old manuscript. Lo trovai cagli occhi fissi sopra un vecchio manoscritto.

— 131 —

VERBI	PREPOS.	ESEMPJ.
To pour Versare.	out.	Shall I pour you out another cup? Vi verserò io un'altra tazza?
—	in.	They are pouring in from every quarter. Entrano in folla da ogni parte.
To prevail Prevalere.	on.	I cannot prevail on him to do it. Non posso persuaderlo di farlo.
—	over.	Might prevails over right. Contro la forza non val ragione.
To put Mettere.	up.	I can no longer put up with your behaviour. Non posso più soffrire la vostra condotta.
—	into.	The ship, in the storm, put into Leghorn. Nella procella la nave approdò a Livorno.
To put Mettere.	out.	Put out the candle. Spegnete la candela.
—	off.	The meeting is put off. La radunanza è prorogata.
—	by.	He puts by what he earns. Pone in serbo quello che guadagna.
To read Leggere.	over.	I have read over the manuscript. Ho letto tutto il manoscritto.
—	out.	Read out. He cries out. Leggete ad alta voce. Egli grida.
To reproach Rimproverare.	with.	I reproached him with his negligence. Gli rimproverai la sua negligenza.
To rub Fregare.	out.	You can rub out that spot. Potete levare quella macchia fregando.
To run Correre.	over.	The bottle runs over. La bottiglia trabocca.
—	through.	He ran him through with his sword. Lo trafisse colla spada.
—	in.	He runs in debt. Contrae molti debiti.
—	one's self out of.	I have run myself out of breath. Mi sono sfiatato correndo.
To set Porre.	about.	I will set about it. Mi accingerò a farlo.
—	down.	Set that down in your book. Notate ciò nel vostro libro.
—	out.	We set out this evening. Partiamo questa sera.
—	on fire.	They set his house on fire. Appiccarono il fuoco alla sua casa.
—	up.	He is set up as a draper. Si è stabilito come fondachiere.
To shift Mutare.	for.	He shifts for himself. Egli fa senz'aiuto altrui.
To stand Stare, reggere.	off, by.	Stand off. I stood by. Fate largo. Io era presente.

VERBI.	PREPOS.	ESEMPI.
—	by.	I will stand by you.
		Vi sosterrò, vi spalleggerò.
—	against.	I can't stand against two.
		Non posso resistere a due.
—	to.	I stand to my word.
		Mantengo la mia parola.
To stare	at.	Why do you stare at me so?
Guardar fisso.		Perché mi guardate cosi fisso fisso?
To slip	out.	I slipped out early.
Sdrucciolare.		Me la svignai (uscii) per tempo.
To squeeze	out.	Squeeze out the juice of that lemon.
Spremere.		Spremete il sugo di quel limone.
To steal	on.	They steal on.
Rubare.		Si avanzano pian pianino.
—	away.	I stole away from the company
		Lasciai la compagnia secretamente.
To step	in, out.	Step in, walk in. He is just stepped out.
Fare un passo.		Entrate, resti servito. È uscito or ora.
To stir.	out.	I am still too weak to stir out.
Muoversi.		Sono ancora troppo debole per uscire.
—	—	My master is not yet stirring.
		Il mio padrone non si è ancora alzato.
To take	away.	We have dined; you may take away.
Prendere.		Abbiamo pranzato; potete sparecchiare.
—	with.	I will take you with me.
		Vi condurrò meco.
—	in.	He has taken you in.
		Vi ha giuntato, gabbato.
—	up.	That takes up too much room.
		Occupa troppo spazio.
—	—	They have taken up the assassins.
		Hanno arrestato gli assassini.
To think	of.	Think of me.
Pensare.		Pensate a me.
To threaten.	with.	He threatened him with death.
Minacciare.		Lo minacciò di morte.
To throw.	at.	Throw a stone at that dog.
Gettare.		Gettate un sasso contro quel cane.
—	out.	He threw out some hints that, etc.
		Egli lasciò capire, diede ad intendere che, ecc.
—	up.	He threw up his employ.
		Diede la sua dimissione.
To trifle	away.	He trifles away his time.
Frascheggiare.		Passa tutto il suo tempo in inezie.
To turn.	away.	He has turned away his valet.
Voltare.		Ha licenziato il suo domestico.
—	into.	He turned him into a tree.
		Egli lo tramutò in un albero.

VERBI	PREPOS.	ESEMPJ.
— —	out.	I will turn you out (put you out). Vi scaccerò fuori.
— —	over.	He is turning over the leaves of your book. Egli trascorre il vostro libro.
—	to.	I turn to you. Mi rivolgo a voi.
— —	down.	Turn down the leaf. Piegate la pagina.
— —	out.	He is turned out a rouge. È divenuto un furbo, ladro.
— —	—	He is turned dancing-master. È divenuto maestro di ballo.
To vie Gareggiare.	with.	They vie with each other. Essi fanno a gara tra loro.

359.

Why have you knocked that man down? It was not I who has knocked him down, it was Mr. Ozioni, because he had taken him in. He had once imposed also upon me, I hear he imposes upon every one, I should like to get acquainted with him, and see if he succeeds in imposing also upon me. I would bet you ten to one, he will. If he will, for my part I will make his conduct known, and thus I will hold him to public scorn. I can't rely upon you, I am afraid you will not abide by your determination, and even if you did you'll never be able to bring it about. I'll answer for it. No man can answer for the futur. He was thought to be very honest and yet he has imposed upon all his friends. I cannot account for it. Nor I neither. His conduct is very strange. He is not alone who don't act up to his principles. He who don't act up to his principles should be despised. Is he very rich? He is said to be a million worth. Did he come by it honestly? I doubt it, I would not confide in him. For my part I was assured he came by it quite honestly. — Where do you board? I board at Mr. Vanni's a very kind gentleman who dotes on her daughter; but

I shall be obliged to look for another boarding house, because poor Mr. Vanni is dying, the doctors have given him over, but let us speak of something else, it pains me to dwel upon this subject.

360.

I francesi hanno attaccato i prussiani e furono battuti. Davvero ? Da chi avete avuto la notizia? L'ho letta nei giornali di questa mattina. Non mi fido dei giornali, non sarebbe la prima volta che dicono menzogne. Spesso ne dicono, è vero, ed io non so darmene una ragione, perchè poi le menzogne si scoprono. Vi ho letto pure una trista notizia, il signor Nulli si è ucciso per disperazione, egli fu ingannato dal suo migliore amico. Come si è ucciso? Si è fatto saltar le cervella. Poveretto da che morì suo figlio egli non faceva altro che pensare alle sue disgrazie. Non si può fidarsi più di nessuno, ognuno tenta d'ingannar l'altro, e Leopardi ha detto bene che il mondo è una guerra di uno contro tutti e di tutti contro uno. Pure ognuno dice che bisogna seguire il bene. Sì, ma pochi agiscono secondo i loro principj. Guardate il signor Beni, ognuno direbbe che egli è giunto all'opulenza onestamente, parla sempre di virtù, pure io so che egli ha ingannato parecchi. Se aveste mantenuto il vostro proposito ognuno vi avrebbe benedetto. Non ha dipeso da me, ha dipeso dalle circostanze se non l'ho mantenuto. Se m'inganna la è finita per me. Vi garantisco il successo purchè non lo diciate a nessuno. È la mia ultima speranza se non riesco, non mi resta altro che farmi saltar le cervella. Non temete, spero di venirne a capo perchè ho a fare con persona che ha sempre agito nobilmente con me, e di cui ci possiamo fidare.

361.

I should like to know why that gentleman stares at me so. It seems he has a great liking with you. I don't care, I don't like to be gazed at. I beg of you to forgive him, he dotes on you. — With what do they charge him? With the crime of murder. Then he will be hanged, will he not? I think so. — Where are you going? I am going out on business, I'll be back soon. Are you still learning german? No, I have given it up, as I found that it took up too much time. What are you peeping through that hole? I am very curious to know something of my cousin's behaviour. Take care my dear, he who peeps through a hole may see what will not please him. — Why are you in such a despair? I want a hundred pounds, and I am at a loss how to find them, help me, pray, do, go to my father and try to persuade him to send me the money. I have already tried, but I could not prevail on him to do it. He says he can no longer put up with your behaviour. — He says lies, he imposes upon his very friends, he has no character at all. He is a very despisable man. Yes, but if you were only to hint at his behaviour, or if you charged him with lying, he would challenge you and very likly would run you through the body, he is a man of honour.

362.

Lo accusano di aver rubato 500 lire sterline a suo zio che lo ama passionatamente, solamente perchè gli aveva rifiutato dieci lire e perchè gli aveva detto francamente che non poteva più soffrire la sua condotta. Chi lo ha scoperto? Una serva che guardava attraverso un buco che c'era nella porta. Voi che siete amico dello zio perchè non tentate di persuaderlo che gli perdoni? Lo farò ma temo non potrò persuaderlo a perdonargli, perchè ora l'odia tanto quanto prima lo amava con passione. Eccolo che viene, non gliene fate cenno vi prego, egli viene da me per affari e non vorrei che andasse in collera meco. — È vero che avete abbandonato lo studio del disegno? Sì,

— 136 —

perchè mi prendeva troppo tempo. Credo piuttosto che siate pigro. Non m'accusate di pigrizia, perchè io sono un uomo d'onore e sarei costretto di trafiggervi colla spada. Non posso soffrire di esser guardata così fisso, volgete altrove gli occhi ve ne prego. Vi prego di perdonarmi, siete così bella che non si può guardar che voi. Siete molto gentile ma se cessaste di dir sciocchezze lo sareste ancora di più.

363.

visitare, *to view*
prendere a salario, *to hire*
ricercare di, *to inquire for*
gabinetto, *closet*

dall'aspetto signorile, *gentlemanly*
chieder scusa, *to apologize*
esser stupito di, *to be astonished at*.

Sebbene avesse chiesto scusa per la sua cattiva condotta, non potè persuadere suo padre a perdonargli, e malgrado le sue lagrime fu chiuso in un gabinetto molto oscuro. Sono stupito di vedervi ancora qui, siccome m'avete detto che sareste partito subito. Avendo preso a salario un servo che è molto intelligente e conosce molto bene la città, sono rimasto per visitarla in sua compagnia. È quello il vostro servo? Sì, è un uomo dall'aspetto signorile, non si direbbe che sia un servo. Di chi ricercate? Sono stupito che voi me lo domandiate, non lo sapete forse? No davvero! Ricerco di quel signore che mi prese a salario e che mi ordinò di trovarmi qui alle cinque e mezzo. È forse un vecchio dall'aspetto signorile? Sì. Egli è in quel gabinetto, uscirà presto, aspettatelo qui. Lasciatemi guardare attraverso il buco per vedere se è lui, ch'io non abbia a perdere il tempo ad aspettarlo inutilmente qui. È vero che l'esercito prussiano si precipitò sul francese? Così si dice. Dicevano anche che Mac Mahon si è fatto saltar le cervella per disperazione, ma era una menzogna. Fummo stupiti udendo che egli

vi aveva chiesto scusa, e che nondimeno lo avete trafitto. Egli lo meritava, m'aveva ingannato parecchie volte,
e s'adirava ogni qualvolta faceva cenno della sua pes-
sima condotta.

364.

he desired the waiter, ordinò al cameriere
to conceive, capire   *the meaning*, il senso
to ascertain, accertarsi   *light*, leggero.

PROVIDENTIAL ESCAPE FROM ASSASSINATION.

Some years ago an Englishman, who was going to make a tour on the continent, landed at Calais, accompanied by only one servant. After staying a few days to view the town and make the necessary preparations for his journey, he hired an additonal servant and fixed the following morning for his departure. As he was sitting at dinner in his own private room, a waiter came and told him that a gentleman wished to speak with him, saying he had something of importance to communicate. The Englishman was much surprised that any one should inquire for him at a place in which he knew nobody; however he desired the waiter to introduce the gentleman.

A very gentlemanly Frenchman was introduced, who, after apologizing for the interruption, said: Sir, I have a communication to make, which is of the greatest importance to you; I am acquainted with all your intentions respecting your journey; I know what money, jewels etc. you have with you, and many other circumstances you will perhaps be astonished at. You are in danger, Sir, in great danger; are you a man of courage? — Your observations, said the Englishman, are indeed very extraordinary; I cannot conceive the meaning of them, but with respects to courage, I hope I shall not be found wanting in a case of necessity; I must however request you to be more explicit. — Well then, Sir, I come to inform you that you are to be robbed and murdered in your bed to night; I am prefect of the police, I am acquainted with the whole plan, and if you have sufficient courage to follow my directions, the robbers will be taken and brought to justice; if not, we can only prevent the execution of their plan. — Well, said the Englishman, what do you wish me to do? — I advise you, said the prefect, to take your accustomed walk after dinner, and not on any account to examine the closets of your bed-room, nor look under your bed before you go to rest; go to bed as usual, feign to sleep and leave the rest to me.

The traveller thanked him, went to take his usual walk, and, having ascertained that it was really the prefect he had seen, returned to his lodging to prepare for the mysterious and alarming event.

After taking a light supper, he retired to his room and shortly went to bed, having followed the instructions he had received. He pretended to be soon asleep, and to sleep very soundly, when, after a short time, he heard something move, and, opening his eyes a little, he perceived two men come out of a closet and approach his bed, one of them having a dark lantern. Our Englishman had sufficient fortitude to remain quiet at his trying moment; the men approached, one of them seized his arms, the other at the same moment was' putting a poniard on his breast, when suddenly, from another closet in the room, rushed four men, police-officers, who seized the murderers almost in the act of assassination. Lights were immediately brought and imagine the Englishman's surprise on recognizing his confidential servant with the poniard in his hand.

Conversation.

What was an Englishman going to make?
Where did he land?
By whom was he accompained?
What did he stay a few days at Calais for?
What day did he fix for his departure?
Who came as he was sitting at dinner?
What was the Englishman surprised at?
Who was introduced?
What did the Frenchman tell the Englishman?
What question did he ask him?
What did the Englishman answer?
What was the Frenchman?
Of what did he inform the Englishman?
What would be the result, if the traveller would follow the Frenchman's directions?
What did the Frenchman consequently advise him to do?
What did the traveller ascertain?
When did he retire to his room?
What did he pretend to be?
Did he hear anything?
Whom did he perceive?
What did the men do?
Did the Englishman remain quiet?
How did the men seize him?
But who rushed from another closet?
At what moment did they seize the murderers?
Whom did the Englishman recognise?

Lezione quarantesima settima. Lesson the forty seventh.

DELLE CONGIUNZIONI.

365.

Oltre gli usi e i sensi delle congiunzioni che l'allievo ha appreso fin qui, conviene notare certi loro peculiari usi e sensi.

as { siccome
      mentre
      come, in qualità di

As my friend was not at home I went away	siccome il mio amico non era in casa me ne andai.
He came in as I was reading	entrò mentre leggeva.
He lived with me as a coachman	stette da me in qualità di cocchiere.
since, poichè	but for, senza
but one, eccetto che uno	but just, appunto or ora
but too, pur troppo	
Since you will not come, I must go by myself	poichè non volete venire me ne andrò da me.
But for him, senza di lui	
We did nothing but laugh	non facemmo che ridere.
He is but just arrived	è arrivato or ora.
The news is but too true	la nuova è pur troppo vera.

Notiamo ancora le seguenti frasi:

Who knows but it may be a lie.	chi sa che non sia una menzogna.
She cannot see tears but she must weep.	non può veder lagrime senza piangere.

Many men live as if they should never die and therefore when death comes, he finds them unprepared and very unwilling to go with him. As you did not come at the fixed hour, I thought you would not come at all. I do not like to tell you the affair that kept me so long, as I know that it would be disagreable to you. And yet I should like to hear it. Since the affair is so, we must leave it so. That poor woman is to be pitied, she has lost all her children but one. So weak are her nerves, that she never hear music but she must weep. How long are you in town? I am but just arrived. I can't bear that young man, he is an idle fellow who has learned nothing but how to spend money. I cannot but allow you are right. They never see each other but they shake hands. Since you wish to learn English you shall have a first-rate master. But for your assistance I should not have done my work. You never touch at any thing but you spoil it.

366.

Poiché gli affari vanno male, ritiratevi, e impiegate il vostro denaro nei fondi. In qualunque maniera lo vorrei implegare fuorché nei fondi pubblici. Avete pur troppo ragione. Non posso pensare alla condotta di mio figlio senza versar lagrime amare. Egli non è buono a nulla eccetto che a giuocare e spender denaro. È uscito or ora, sarà andato a giocare coi suoi amici. Venite meco, siccome ho tempo, voglio andare a rimproverargli la sua cattiva condotta. Non posso, ora devo uscire per affari. Poiché non volete venire ci andrò solo. Chi sa che non lo incontriate per istrada. Tanto meglio. Chi sa che non si penta e non voglia correggersi. Povero me, la è finita per me, ho perduto tutti i miei amici eccetto che uno, e anche quello è lontano da me. Non so che cosa abbia attorno di me, vostro cugino non face che ridere quando andai a trovarlo. Chi sa che non abbia riso per lo strano cappello che avete in testa. Senza di esso prenderei certo un raffreddore.

367.

Le congiunzioni negative *neither nor* si adoprano anche indipendentemente l'una dall'altra e allora significano *neanche* p. o. :

The weather is bad, nor is there much hope of its being fine. Il tempo è cattivo, neanche c'è speranza che diventi bello.

to have a sore foot, aver male a un piede
confinement, reclusione, ritiro
tediousness, noia   *to afford,* fornire
sore eyes, occhi ammalati   *to lighten,* alleggerire
to have sore eyes, aver male agli occhi.

The child is dangerously ill, nor is there any hope of its recovery. I can't go out, as I have a sore foot, nor have I any book to lighten the tediousness of my confinement. Couldn't you afford me any means to lighten it? Really I don't know. I saw your father and I assured him you were well, but he said, he could scarcely believe it, for if it were, you would certainly have written him. — Do you know where is Mr Belli's abode? I don't know it, neither did I ever know it. What would you advise to lighten the tediousness of such long evening? I would go to theatre but I haven't got any box. But for my sore eyes I would read some amusing book.

368.

È uscito quest'oggi vostro fratello ? No signore e neanche uscirà per quindici giorni, ha male a un piede ed è obbligato al ritiro, egli mi pregò di venire da voi, per vedere se poteste fornirgli qualche buon libro, acciò possa alleggerire la noia della sua reclusione. Mi rincresce non ho alcun libro a mia disposizione, e neanche conosco nessuno che potesse fornirmene, ma verrò a trovarlo e passeremo qualche ora in buona compagnia, cosi potrà sopportare la noia del suo ritiro. Se non avessi malo agli occhi vorrei scrivere la mia storia, ciò mi servirebbe anche per alleggerire la noia delle lunghe sere d'inverno.

369.

ere now, prima d'ora *loan*, prestito.

Requesting the Loan of some Books during Sickness (*).

London, 4th June, 18—.

DEAR——,—I am far from well; indeed, I have been confined to my sofa for some days past, and have enjoyed no amusement but such as my few books afforded me. I write to beg the loan of some of the " Waverley " novels, of which I know you possess a complete set. They shall be taken every possible care of, and returned as regularly as read. Pray look in for an hour now and then, and speak a few words of comfort to

        Yours ever sincerely,

To Miss——.   (——).

The Answer.

Courzon Street, June 4th, 18—.

DEAR——,—How grieved I am to hear of your illness! I send you half a dozen volumes, which I hope will lighten the tediousness of your sofa-confinement, and will come and see you to-morrow morning. I should have done so ere now, but have been so variously engaged, that I have scarcely had a minute to myself.

Wishing sincerely to find you better,

      I am,

       Dear——,

      Yours ever affectionately,

To Miss——.   (——).

(*) Per richiedere in prestito qualche libro durante la malattia.

370.

perder di vista uno, *to lose sight of one*   totale, *utter* allegrezza, *cheerfulness*
stimolo, *sting*.

Poichè non avete nulla da fare, saliamo quella collina, vi si gode una magnifica vista. Non ci sono stato che una volta e non ricordo la via. Non importa, venite dietro a me, ma badate di non perdermi di vista. A proposito che n'è divenuto del nostro povero Giovanni? Per correr dietro agli stimoli dell'ambizione egli perdette di vista i suoi veri interessi e quelli della sua famiglia e fu ridotto in totale miseria. Poichè siete suo amico e lo amate perchè non avete tentato di metterlo sulla buona via? I buoni consigli non sono mai ascoltati mio caro. Pur troppo avete ragione .... L'allegrezza è la salute dell'anima. Non dimenticate quel povero Francesco, neanche perdete di vista il nostro affare, chè se non riesce siamo in totale rovina.

371.

to stick, attaccare	*stuck* stuck
alehouse, birraria	*footman*, valetto
to wander about, andar girando intorno·	*pond*, stagno
	saucepan, casserola
donkey, somaro	*cottage*, capanna
advertisement, annunzio	*bill*, manifesto.

THE LOST CHILD FOUND.

Lady Montagu, being at her country seat as usual in the summer, used to send her little boy Edward to walk every day with the footman, who had strict orders never to lose sight of him. One day however the servant, meeting an old acquaintance, went into an alehouse to drink and left the little boy running about by himself. After staying some time drinking, the footman came out to look for the child to take him home to dinner, but he could not find him. He wandered about till night, inquiring at every cottage and at every house, but in vain, no Edward could be found. The poor mother, as may well be imagined, was in the greatest anxiety about the absence of her dear boy, but, it would be impossible to describe her grief and despair, when the footman returned and told her he did not know what had become of him.

People were sent to seek him in all directions, advertisements were put in all the newspapers; bills were stuck up in London and in most of the great towns of England, offering a considerable reward to any person who would bring him or give any news of him. All endeavours were however unsuccessful, and it was concluded that the poor child had fallen into some pond, or that he had been stolen by gipsies, who would not bring him back for fear of being punished.

Lady Montagu passed long years in this wretched uncertainty, she did not return to London as usual in the winter, but passed her time in grief and solitude in the country. At length a sister of hers married, and, after many refusals, lady Montagu consented to give a ball and supper on the occasion at her town-house, she went to London to superinted the preparations, and while the supper was cooking, the whole house was alarmed by a cry of: fire !

It appears that one of the cooks had overturned a saucepan, and set fire to the chimney. The chimneysweepers were sent for, and a little boy was sent up; but the smoke nearly suffocated him, and he fell into the fire-place. Lady Montagu came herself with some vinegar and a smelling bottle; she began to bathe his temples and his neck, when she suddenly screamed out: Oh ! Edward ! — and fell senseless on the floor. She soon recovered, and taking the little sweeper in her arms, pressed him to her bosom, crying: It is my dear Edward! It is my lost boy!

It appears she had recognised him by a mark on his neck. The master-chimney-sweeper, on being asked where he had obtained the child, said he had bought him about a year before of a gipsy-woman, who said he was her son. All that the boy could remember was, that some people had given him fruit, and told him they would take him home to his mamma; but that they took him a long way, upon a donkey and after keeping him a long while, they told him he must go and live with the chimney-sweeper, who was his father; that they had beaten him so much, whenever he spoke of his mamma and of his fine house, that he was almost afraid to think of it. But he said his master, the chimney-sweeper, had treated him very well.

Lady Montagu rewarded the man handsomely, and from that time she gave every year a feast to all the chimney-sweepers of the Metropolis, on the first of May, the birth-day of little Edward, and now the first of May is still celebrated as the chimney-sweepers' holiday.

Conversation.

Where was lady Montagu in the summer?
What did she use to do with little Edward?
What orders had the footman?
Whom did one day the servant meet?
Where did he go then and where did he leave the boy?
Did he find him again when coming out?
What did he do then?
How did the poor mother feel, when she heard what had happened?
What did she do then?

Was it of any use ?
What did they conclude then ?
How long did lady Montagu pass in that uncertainty ?
Did she return to London in the winter?
On what reason did she consent to give a ball ?
To what purpose did she go to London ?
By what was the house alarmed ?
How had fire been set to the chimney ?
Who was sent for ?
What happened with the little boy who was sent up ?
What did lady Montagu do, and what happened ?
How did she recognise her son ?
What did the chimney-sweeper say about the child ?
What could the boy remember ?
How, did he say, the master-sweeper had treated him ?
How did lady Montagu reward the man ?
What did she give every year ?
As what is the first of May celebrated ?

Lezione quarantesima ottava.   Lesson the forty eighth.

Dell'Ellissi, Inversioni, e delle Terminazioni che modificano il senso e cambiano la natura della parola.

372.

In generale l'ellissi è permessa od usata nella lingua inglese ogni qual volta essa non nuoce alla chiarezza della frase.

Oltre l'ellissi che già conosciamo dell'articolo o aggettivo possessivo avanti a più nomi che si seguono retti dallo stesso articolo o aggettivo possessivo, del pronome relativo, della congiunzione o del segno verbale innanzi a più verbi allo stesso modo e tempo, si usa elidere:

1° La preposizione che si ripete avanti a più regimi.
2° Dopo alcuni verbi si usa elidere la preposizione da essi retta p. e.:

to attain to   to pray to
to catch at   to prevent from
to meet with   to repent of.

3° Quando in una frase di due membri, tutti due i membri si riferiscono allo stesso soggetto, allora dopo le parole, *while, when, if, though*, si elide tanto il pronome personale che il verbo *essere*, p. e.:

Proud men never have friends; WHEN RICH, *because they know nobody;* WHEN POOR *because nobody knows them.*

4° Dopo *as* si può elidere il pronome neutro impersonale *it*, p. e.:

As appears, come apparisce.

5° Dopo alcune preposizioni si elide il verbo *to have* seguito dal participio passato, e allora questo diventa participio presente, p. e.:

after taking, dopo aver preso
before going, prima di esser andato.

to attain one's aim, ottenere lo scopo
to envy, invidiare
to worship, adorare
ten fold, dieci volte tanto
affected, affettato.

Men, if happy, should think of others; if rich, should give to others, and though poor should avoid envying others. — Do you wish to understand how a great man come to be worshipped as a hero, remember what time can do; remember how if a man was great when living, he becomes ten fold greater when dead. — If things are not done here as well as could be wished, they are at least done as well as could be expected from such people. — You are wrong to complain with your son, he has done as much progress as could be expected from one of his years. After taking six months lessons he speaks french tolerably well. I met him yesterday at half past six and he was studying. I don't think he will ever attain his aim as he is too lazy.

373.

Le stesse maniere che stanno bene quando sono naturali, rendono ridicoli quando sono affettate. Se siete povero avrete pochi amici, se ricco avrete molti nemici. Dopo averlo insultato lo sfidò; e dopo averlo trafitto pianse amaramente sulla di lui morte. Come apparisce da questo documento voi gli dovete cinque mila lire, e siccome pare egli ne abbia bisogno mi mandò a pregarvi che vogliate saldare i conti con lui. Dopo avermi ingannato voleva farmi credere alla sua amicizia, e quando l'incontrai volea stringermi la mano. Dovreste aver più cura dell'educazione dei vostri figli, poichè se saranno poveri servirà loro per guadagnarsi da vivere, se ricchi per godere la vita. — Non posso sopportare la pigrizia di quel ragazzo; dopo aver preso un anno di lezione di lingua inglese non sa ancora scrivere una lettera senza errori, so voi volete che divenga qualche cosa di buono bisogna che prendiate più cura di lui, altrimenti non raggiungerete mai il vostro scopo.

374.

Quando nel soggiuntivo passato si sopprimo la congiunziono *if* il verbo si mette prima del soggetto.

Were I you, se io fossi in voi.

Should, avanti al soggetto valo ancho pel presente Indicativo e imperfetto del soggiuntivo, p. e.:

Should I have, { se ho
{ se avessi.

S'inverte la costruzione ancho dopo *what* o *how* esclamativi; *never, on no,* p. o.:

never was I here

base, vile   *to starve,* morir di fame
to dismiss, licenziare   *to do wrong,* fare ingiustizia
to look to, rivolgersi a   *dull,* stupido.

Had I supposed you capable of such ingratitude, you should have starved ere I would have assisted you. — Were I you I should dismiss such a man from my service. Should I discover any thing wrong, I shall of course look to you for satisfaction. Should they deceive us, it would be no hard matter to find them out. What a beautiful girl is she! How do I love her! On no occasion do I find myself so dull as when I am near her. Never in my life did I feel such a transport as for her.— Should I be in want I would look to you for assistance. Should I dismiss him would you enter in my service? Very willingly. Never had I refused him assistance, and look how ungrateful he is.

375.

Se fossi in voi non permetterei a mio figlio di andare con un uomo così cattivo. Egli assicura che gli fanno ingiustizia, che è stato sempre onesto, ma disgraziato. Se anche giurasse che gli fanno ingiustizia non vi affrettate a credergli. Mi ha dato la sua parola che sarebbe venuto a trovarmi alle dieci e mezzo. Se anche manca alla sua parola non ci perdete nulla, credete a me. Io non lo posso soffrire, io lo odio, e se anche morisse di fame non lo aiuterei. Mai in mia vita mi sono incontrato con un uomo così ingrato, e se avessi supposto in lui un' anima così vile, prima avrebbe potuto morir di fame che ottenere la mia pietà. In nessuna occasione mi rivolgerei a voi, so che mai avreste pietà di me, e se anche morissi di fame non mi aiutereste.

376.

TERMINAZIONI CHE MODIFICANO IL SENSO O CAMBIANO LA NATURA DELLA PAROLA.

I sostantivi diventano aggettivi od avverbi mediante l'aggiunta delle terminazioni:

ly, y, less, ful, some, ish.

ly e *y*, acconna la somiglianza o il possesso delle qualità espresse dalla parola radicale, p. e.:

father, padre   *fatherly,* paterno (da padre)
man, uomo   *manly,* da uomo
might, potenza   *mighty,* potente (con potenza)
dust, polvere   *dusty,* polveroso.

less, acconna la privazione, la mancanza della qualità espressa dalla parola radicale, p. e.:

hope, speranza   *hopeless,* senza speranza
end, fine   *endless,* senza fine.

ful, non è altro che l'aggettivo *full* tolto una *l*; indica l'abbondanza, la pienezza, la disposizione a produrre, p. e.:

care, cura
beauty, bellezza

careful, accurato
beautiful, bello (pieno di bellezza).

some, questa terminazione si aggiunge anche agli aggettivi ed avverbi; indica puro il possesso della qualità espressa dalla parola radicale, p. e.:

trouble, disturbo

troublesome, disturboso.

ish, aggiunto agli aggettivi è quasi diminutivo e dispregiativo, aggiunto ai nomi fa l'istesso ufficio che la terminazione *ly*, p. e.:

sweet, dolce
red, rosso
child, fanciullo

sweetish, dolcigno
reddish, rossiccio
childish, fanciullesco.

hood, questa desinenza s'unisce tanto agli aggettivi che ai sostantivi; indica un carattere, una maniera d'essere, p. e.:

false, falso
neighbour, vicino

falsehood, falsità
neighbourhood, vicinanza.

ness, unito all'aggettivo forma il nome astratto, p. e.:

sweet, dolce

sweetness, dolcezza.

ship, unito ai nomi e qualche volta anche agli aggettivi, indica la condizione, p. e.:

friend, amico
dictator, dittatore

friendship, amicizia
dictatorship, dittatura.

en, unito a molti aggettivi, ne forma il verbo, p. e.:

black, nero
wide, largo
light, leggero

to blacken, annerire
to widen, allargare
to lighten, alleggerire.

Talvolta avviene che ad un sostantivo sono unite due di queste desinenze come nella parola:

artlessness cioè art, arte, artless, senza arte, artlessness, ingenuità.

Be careful if you wish to be happy, if you go on and be so careless as you have been till now, you shall come to nothing in the world and by your carelessness you shall turn a penniless and friendless fellow. You are very troublesome my dear, you had better think of yourself, do you immagine perhaps you are faultless? No, I do not, but I am sure, I am not such a childish fellow as you are. By the by, did you put the question to Miss Julia? Yes, and she answered me with all the artlessness of youth and innocence that she could not love me because she was in love with someone else. Do you know with whom? Yes, with that poor fatherless Charles; I like her so much the more for the sweetness of her temper. Then you must be satisfied with her friendship. It is but too true, but I am not quite hopeless. How so? I will not tell it you.

377.

Senza padre e madre, senza speranza e senza denari sono abbandonato nel mondo, che ne sarà di me? I mezzi di guadagnar denaro onestamente sono senza fine, e con cura e industria pieno d'ingegno come siete potrete anche voi farvi una posizione nella società. Io pure era senza aiuto ma pieno di speranza e di coraggio, ho saputo acquistarmi l'amicizia e la stima di chi mi conobbe. Il vostro fanciullesco contegno mi fa disperare. Lo dite proprio sul serio? Certamente, in tutta la vicinanza non si parla che della debolezza del mio carattere perché non so frenare la vostra fierezza.

378.

Caro signore, il mio padrone è molto in collera con me perché me ne sono andato senza aver chiuso la porta di casa, temo che mi licenzi, sebbene io sia da dieci anni al suo servizio e mai finora si sia lamentato di me; se mi licenziasse potrei rivolgermi a voi per trovare un altro padrone? Se è vero ciò che mi dite e che il vostro padrone vi licenziasse, rivolgetevi pure a me ed io vi aiuterò, ma se egli vi accusa di qualche altra mancanza rivolgetevi ad altri, io non son disposto ad aiutare chi non lo merita. Entro otto giorni vi darò la risposta, in ogni modo venite a trovarmi subito che potete, perchè può darsi che riceva notizie anche prima. Non vi lamentate degli altri, pensate alla vostra condotta, e vedrete che sarete trattato come voi trattate, se siete buono sarete amato, se cattivo odiato. Avete perfettamente ragione, però accade qualche volta che si è odiati senza aver fatto nulla di male, e che si è amati senza averlo meritato.

379.

bag, sacco
taproom, sala di osteria, birraria
they are making a fool of you, si burlano di voi
to contrive, riuscire
to loap, saltare

public house, birraria
by the powers, per Dio !
wag, burlone
on all fours, su quattro zampe.

THE DOUBLE METAMORPHOSIS.

An Irishman was once employed, by a gentleman at Hampstead, to carry a live hare, as a present, to one of his friends at London. It was put into a bag, and he set off. Hampstead being about five miles from London, the Irishman stopped half way at a public house, to rest himself, and to drink a pint of beer. Some wags, who were drinking in the taproom, finding what he had in the bag determined to play him a trick and one of them, while the others kept him in conversation, took out the hare and put in a cat.
Having finished his beer, the Irishman started with

his load. On arriving at London, he said to the gentleman; Sir, my master has sent you a live hare. — Very well, said he, let us see it. — He then opened the sack and to his great astonishment found a cat. — By the powers ! said Paddy it was at hare at Hampstead, for I saw it put into the bag. — Go back, go back, said the gentleman, they are making a fool of you. — Paddy took up the bag, and trotted off again towards Hampstead, stopping, on his return, at the same public house, and telling his adventure, to the amusement of those who had played him the trick. To render the farce complete they contrived to take out the cat and replace the hare; and the unsuspecting Irishman set off again for Hampstead.

On arriving, he said to his master, Sir, do you know that you have sent a cat instead of a hare? — Go along, you stupid fellow, replied the gentleman, — Well, then, believe your own eyes. — On saying which, he opened the bag, and out leaped the hare. The Irishman could scarcely believe his eyes and appeared for some moments petrified with fear: at length he ejaculated, by Jasus, it is a hare at Hampstead, and a cat at London ! — Come, come, said the master, put it into the bag and return. — By Jasus, master, I shall go no more, for if the wile air of London can change a hare into a cat, it may, perhaps, change me into an ass; and will I, think you, risk going on all fours during the rest of my days?

Lezione quarantesima nona. — Lesson the forty ninth.

FRASEOLOGIA.

380.

by all means, in tutti i casi
by no means, in nessun caso
it is not worth while speaking, non vale la pena di parlarne
to stop payment, sospendere i pagamenti
how much on the hundred will he pay? quanto per cento pagherà?
fifty on the hundred, cinquanta per cento
to be in a fine mess, trovarsi in un bell'impiccio
upon the whole, al postutto
glass, with care, posa-piano
within reach of, alla portata di
within myself, tra me e me
within reach of hearing } alla portata di udire
within hearing
to fell sick } cader ammalato
to be taken ill
to ring (rang, rung) the bell, suonar il campanello
to call in question, metter in dubbio
as it were, per così dire
by little and little, a poco a poco
lately married, sposi di fresco
worth his weight in gold, vale tant'oro quanto pesa
to go arm in arm, andar a braccetto
every thing topsy turvy, ogni cosa sossopra
to take the hint, mangiar la foglia .

investment, investimento, collocazione
to be hand and glove, essere due anime in un nocciolo
underhand, di sottomano, di nascosto
I can't find it in my heart, non mi dà il cuore
too much of one thing is good for nothing, il soverchio rompe il coperchio
be off, alla larga
to be in a right frame of mind, esser ben disposto
don't rekon your chickens before they are hatched, non dir quattro se non l'hai nel sacco
beyond all bounds, oltre ogni limite
in a trice, subito, in un attimo
the stocks, i fondi pubblici   *step*, gradino.

It is scarcely worth while for me to speak to you about that money which I lent you, but you should by no means forget it, and since you have got yourself in such a fine mess with your R. R. (*) stock, I will be more indulgent with you. By the way, when did the Company stop payment and how much upon the whole did you receive on the hundred for your investment?

At first I got ten per cent, but afterwards falling sick myself that I could not attend to it and the underhand dealing of the directors reduced this dividend by little and little to nothing as it were. For a long time I did not call in question the honesty of the directors and even considered every soul of them worth his weight in gold, but when I saw in their report, the expenses beyond all bounds of moderation and the affairs of the Company all topsy-turvy, I took the hint, and one day when in a right frame of mind for it, I said within myself "too much of the thing is good for nothing" and was off in a trice to sell the whole of my interest. Going

---

(*) Abbreviativo di *Rail-Road*.

down to the Exchange I saw on the door-steps of his house one of my acquaintances, who was lately married, arm in arm with his beautiful lady who had just rung the bell to enter, so approaching quickly within hearing, I called out to him to stop by all means a moment. He turned round, descended the steps as carefully as one would a box marked, "Glass, with care!" and when within reach of me gave me, his hand asking, "what news?" I told him my trouble and asked his advice, but the poor fellow was all hand and glove in love and declared he couldn't find it in his heart to counsel me, but said however, if he were in my place the next time he invested his money he would not count his chickens before they were hatched.

381.

Sapete nulla dei cugini Franceschi ? è molto tempo che non li veggo, e ne sono alquanto inquieto perchè m'avevano detto che il più giovane era caduto ammalato. Vi posso assicurare che stanno perfettamente bene tutti due, li ho veduti questa mattina che andavano a braccetto come il loro solito. Che cosa intendete di dire? Non sapete che sono due anime in un nocciolo? Mettereste forse in dubbio la loro amicizia? No davvero; ma mi hanno fatto troppo male perchè possa amarli. Che cosa vi hanno fatto? Non sapete che mi hanno rovinato? Davvero? Dopo due mesi che io aveva confidato loro i miei risparmi hanno sospeso i pagamenti, e dovetti accontentarmi del venti per cento. Io sapeva che avevano sospeso i pagamenti ma credeva che avessero pagato il cinquanta per cento; e al postutto non credo che per aver sospeso i pagamenti, meritino di esser disprezzati. Anzi valgono tant'oro quanto pesano, poveretti. Non siete ben disposto quest'oggi, è inutile parlar con voi. E come potrei esserlo? — Chi ha messo ogni cosa sossopra nella mia stanza? Non andate in collera, è stato mio figlio, perdonategli, vi prego. Io gli perdono volentieri, ma se non lo battete di quando in quando, egli diventerà a poco a poco così fiero che non potrete sopportare la sua condotta. Avete ragione, ma non mi dà il cuore di batterlo, temo che s'ammali, non vedete come egli è delicato, pare abbia scritto in fronte: « Posa-piano. » — Siete troppo indulgente con lui, e sapete il proverbio: il soverchio rompe il coperchio. — Non so darmi ragione della tua pazza allegrezza, che cosa ti è accaduto? Non sai la notizia? Mio zio che era ricchissimo mi ha fatto erede di tutti i suoi beni. Caro mio, non dir quattro se non l'hai nel sacco; se tuo zio ha lasciato molto denaro egli può anche aver lasciato molti debiti. Come? tu metti in dubbio la sua ricchezza? Non metto in dubbio nulla io, ma non bisogna far il conto senza l'oste, e se egli ha lasciato molti debiti come mi dicono, tu potresti trovarti in un bell'impiccio. Io spero che non mi troverò in alcun impiccio, e se divento ricco ti assicuro che saprò mostrarti la mia gratitudine per la bontà che hai avuta per me finora. Oh non vale la pena di parlarne; io ti desidero ogni bene e ti prego di continuarmi la tua amicizia.

382.

explanation, spiegazione   lip, labbra
bush, cespuglio   feathers, piume, penne.
slip, fallo, caso

A bird in the hand is worth two in the bush. Do you know that proverb? It means that you must never give up a thing that you have, to look out for another that you will perhaps never get. Many a man would not be unhappy, if he had always thought of that proverb. Another proverb is this: "There is many a slip between the cup and the lip. That means, that you can never be sure of having a thing, till you hold it in your hands or in your mouth; because you may lose it before it comes into your possession. Another is this: An old dog learns no tricks. It means, that you must learn when young, that in your later years you cannot learn so well as in your youth. Another that wants no explanation, is: Early to bed and early to rise, makes a man healthy, wealthy, and wise. The English say of a man, that borrows money of one to pay another: He robs Peter to pay Paul. Do not spend your money in trifles, a penny saved is a penny won. Did you see Mr. Fox at the concert last night? Yes, he was dressed quite elegantly; I hardly knew him. He has won some money in the lottery and thinks: Fine feathers make fine birds. He knows on which side his bread is buttered; he is going to marry a rich lady, who loves him very much. If he cannot get her, I fear he will be ruined. He is an idle fellow who has learned nothing but how to spend money. It seems you do not like him much. Well, we shall see. All is well that ends well.

383.

Non sprecate il vostro tempo in frivolezze mentre siete giovani perchè da vecchi si apprende difficilmente, neanche lasciate sfuggir le occasioni di guadagnar poco per la speranza di guadagnar molto in avvenire, perchè val più un uovo oggi che una gallina domani; abituatevi anche a coricarvi di buon'ora e levarvi per tempo perchè chi dorme non piglia pesci. Badate anche a non preferir l'apparenza alla sostanza, a stimar un uomo per il suo elegante vestito o a sprezzarlo se è male abbigliato, perchè ricordatevi che l'abito non fa il monaco. Voi mi annoiate coi vostri proverbi. Eppure essi sono la sapienza del popolo. Non servono però a trar d'impiccio un povero uomo come me. No, ma servono ad evitare di trovarsi in impiccio; e se voi aveste pensato al proverbio, che non bisogna far il conto senza l'oste, non vi trovereste oggi in un tal impiccio; soprattutto se vi foste ricordato che un soldo risparmiato vale uno guadagnato, non vi trovereste oggi costretto a cercar denari in prestito da coloro che credete vostri amici e che trovate senza compassione. Pur troppo avete ragione, mi pento amaramente di aver avuto confidenza negli uomini, perchè non sapeva che essi raramente agiscono secondo i loro principii. Spero che la lezione vi servirà questa volta e che in avvenire non avrete più una confidenza così cieca nell'amicizia degli uomini, acciò non abbiano a burlarsi di voi. Non dubitate, ho recitato abbastanza la parte dell'agnello, voglio vedere se mi riesce di rappresentare quella del lupo.

384.

Modelli di biglietti.

N.B. Nei biglietti gl'Inglesi usano parlar di sè e della persona a cui scrivono in terza persona.

D'invito.

Mr. and Mrs. Smith present their most respectful compliments to Mr. and Mrs. Black and request the honour of their company to dinner on Monday at five o'clock.

Mr. and Mrs. Black present their respects to Mr. and Mrs. Smith, and will not fail accepting their kind invitation.

Risposta negativa.

Mr. and Mrs. Black's compliments to Mr. and Mrs. Smith, and are very sorry that a previous engagement for Monday will prevent their having the honor of waiting upon them that day.

Il signor Rapi presenta il suo rispetto al sig. Levi, gli rincresce di non poter prendere mercoledì la lezione di tedesco. Il sig. Levi avrà la gentilezza di venire venerdì secondo il solito.

Mr. Salom presents his compliments to Mr. and Mrs. Johnson, and begs that they will not give themselves the trouble of calling upon him this evening, as he finds himself obliged to go into the country to-morrow and will be very glad to see Mr. and Mrs. Johnson on the same evening.

La signorina Wellington manda i suoi saluti alla signora Barcia, e la prega di venire con le sue figlie a passare da lei la sera di giovedì. Vi sarà compagnia e il tempo passerà allegramente.

La signora Barcia ringrazia e saluta la gentile signorina Wellington, e le rincresce di non poter venire a passare in così lieta compagnia la sera di giovedì, a causa di un antecedente impegno.

Biglietti per chiedere un abboccamento.

Mr. Stewart's respectful compliments to Mr. Darmont, and desires to know the day and hour he may call upon him, having something of great consequence to acquaint him with (¹). Mr. Stewart hopes that Mr. Darmont will excuse his importunity.

Mr. Shawcross requests Professor Wilson will have the kindness to call on him to-morrow morning at any hour before 11, as he wishes to speak with him about English lessons, for his daughter.

(¹) Da trattar con lui.

Lezione cinquantesima.   Lesson the fiftieth.

FRASEOLOGIA COMMERCIALE.

385.

MANIERE DI COMINCIARE LE LETTERE COMMERCIALI.

Signor! *Sir, Dear Sir*	Signori, *Gentlemen.*
Abbiamo il piacere di accusare la grata vostra del 10 corrente (andante, volgente).	*We have the pleasure to acknowledge the receipt of your favor of the 10 instant.*
Del primo dello scorso mese.	*of 1st, ultimo*
Siamo senza favorite vostre a riscontrare.	*We have none of your esteemed favors unanswered.*
Scopo precipuo della presente si è.	*Our principal motive of addressing you is.*
Approfitto di questa occasione particolare onde rispondere alla cara vostra.	*I avail myself of this privy occasion to reply to your favor.*
Confermandovi l'ultima mia dei . . .	*Confirming my last respects of . . .*
Abbiamo sott'occhio le pregiate vostre lettere.	*Your esteemed favours are by us.*
Conformemente al desiderio espressomi coll'ultima vostra.	*Agreeable to the wish expressed in the last letter we had the pleasure to receive from you.*

MANIERE DI FINIRE LE LETTERE COMMERCIALI.

In attesa di vostre nuove, vi salutiamo con perfetta stima.	*Waiting your further favor, we are with esteem, Sir,*
	your obedient humble servant (che si scrive in abbreviazione): *your obt. hble, svts.*
Ho l'onore di dirmi con ogni devozione, vostro affezionatissimo	*I have the honour of subscribing myself, ever your most affectionately.*
In attesa di una pronta — sollecita risposta — pronto — sollecito riscontro, ho l'onore.	*Hoping you will favour me with an early reply to the present, I remain.*
Vi prego di accogliere l'assicurazione della mia profonda stima.	*I remain with much esteem and regard...*
Senz'altro dirvi, vi salutiamo con distinta stima e considerazione,	*Without further, we are, with great regard, Gentlemen, your mo. obt. svts.*
Non avendo altro a comunicarvi pel momento, vi salutiamo affettuosamente.	*Having nothing more to trouble you with, we remain respectfully,*
In tutta fretta vi salutiamo.	*We remain in haste....*
Abbiate la bontà — compiacenza d'incamminare — inoltrare l'inchiusa — l'acclusa al suo indirizzo — al suo destino, per maggiormente obbligare il vostro devotissimo...	*Please to forward the enclosed letter — the enclosure to its address — destination, and oblige, your most obedient servant.*

Scusato — perdonate il disturbo — l'imbarazzo — la pena — la briga che vi arrechiamo — cagioniamo, e credeteci i vostri devotissimi...	Please excuse this trouble and believe us, cordialy yours...
Riapro — dissuggello la presente — la lettera per comunicarvi — per darvi avviso — per indicarvi che...	I open this letter after its having been sealed in order to advise you of — to communicate you that.

AFFARI IN GENERALE.

Intendersela su di un affare...	To agree to business, to come to an understanding about a business ...
Gli affari si presentano bene — vanno bene ...	Business is going on well...
Gli affari sono animati ...	Business is animated-brisk.
Finire un affare ...	To bring about a business...
Pesare l'affare — riflettere maturamente sopra un affare ...	To consider maturely about a business ...
Quest'affare avrà un esito sfortunato — infelice.	This transaction — business will turn out badly — unfortunately.
Abbiamo pochi affari ...	There is not much stir in business ...
... siccome una grande attività regna nelle fabbriche, vi è tutta l'apparenza che gli affari tosto riprenderanno ...	... As the manufacturing trade continues very brisk, we may shortly look for a revival ...

Affari del momento — della giornata . . .	The business doing . . .
. . . dimodochè gli affari procedono ben tristamente. . .	. . . so that business goes on very indifferently indeed . . .
Vi sono infinitamente obbligato degli avvisi che mi dato sull'andamento della vostra piazza assicurandovi che la loro continuazione mi riescirà molto gradita . . .	I am indebted to you for your quotations of your market, and shall feel myself obliged for its continuation . . .
Gli affari vanno a gonfie vele . . .	Business is in full activity...
Vi è stato dell'aumento pronunciato nei prezzi delle operate transazioni . . .	All business transacted — done was at decidedly higher rates . . .

Nomenclatura di merci.

ambra, *ambergis*
amido, *starch*
asfalto, *aspalt*
cuoio e pelli preparate, *leather*
filati o fili, *yarn or twist*
gesso, *plaster*
legname di costruzione o da tornio, *timber and cabinet wood*
legumi, *pulse*
olio di lino, *thym e oil*
pece, *pitch*
pelliccerie, *peltry-furs*

canapi, *hemp*
cannella, *cinnamon*
cuoio o pelli, *hides*
gomma, *gum*
lana, *wool*
polpa di cassia, *cassia sticks*
sego, *tallow*
spezierie, *spices*
traliccio, *diaper*.

386.

(Circular.)

To Messrs. N. N.

London, Jan. 1, 1847.

Gentlemen,

We have the honour of informing you, that we have formed a partnership[1], under the firm[2] of B. and Co. for the transacting of general commission business[3]; and when favourable opportunities occur[4], we may be induced to speculate for our own or joint account[5]; giving then, of course[6], a preference to such houses as[7] favour us with their commands in this quarter[8]. Respecting our solidity, integrity and knowledge of business in general, and our full competency to further[9] the interests of our correspondents, we beg to refer you[10] to Messrs. A. and B. C. and D. and K. and Co. all of this city, who will satisfy any inquiries you may choose[11] to make with regard to us. Be pleased to note[12] our respective signatures. We are, &c.

Geo. B.: B. and Co.
Tred. L.: B. and Co.

[1] società
[2] ditta
[3] per trattare affari di commissione in generale
[4] si presentassero
[5] per nostro proprio conto o per conto sociale
[6] naturalmente
[7] e quelle case che
[8] piazza
[9] idoneità a promuovere
[10] vi preghiamo di rivolgervi
[11] qualsivoglia inchiesta che crediate opportuno
[12] compiacetevi di prender nota.

To Messrs. K. and Co. St. Petersburgh.

London, Jan. 5, 1847.

Gentlemen,

We return[1] our best thanks for the great attention you were pleased[2] to show our Mr. L. during his stay[3]

[1] vi facciamo
[2] premura che vi compiaceste
[3] soggiorno

in your city. As¹ it frequently happens, that a confidential agent on the spot⁵ may be of infinite service in the recovery of dubious debts⁶ &c., be assured, that, should you ever require⁷ our mediation in that or any other way, we shall make it⁸ our first object to attend to your interest. Upon considering all circumstances, we are of opinion, that the present moment offers a favourable prospect for consignments to and from your place. Annexed, we beg leave to hand you⁹ our price current, which, when compared with yours, will fully enable you¹⁰ to judge the article that would turn to advantage¹¹, in this or your market. It appears that tallow, according to your price-current, might turn¹² to a good speculation; for it is quoted¹³ at 50 rubles per pound, and sells here at £ 4..5..0 per cwt¹⁴.

Hemp and flax are much in demand¹⁵, but in corn we would not advise you¹⁶ to speculate, as the market here is quite overstocked¹⁷.

We recommend ourselves to your friendship, and are with respect, &c.   B. and Co.

⁴ siccome
⁵ lungo
⁶ ricupero di crediti mal sicuri
⁷ assicuratevi che se mai richiedente
⁸ qualunquealtroemergente, sarà
⁹ vi trasmettiamo
¹⁰ vi porrà perfettamente in grado di
¹¹ che riescirebbe vantaggioso
¹² potrebbe risultare
¹³ segnato
¹⁴ continuò (hundred weight)
¹⁵ ricerca
¹⁶ non vi consiglieremmo
¹⁷ soverchiamente provvisto.

To Lubec.

London.

We refer you to our respects of the..., advising¹ the execution of part of your order, yet, as the late² unexpected alteration in politics has had a great effect

¹ vi confermiamo la nostra del..., che vi annunziava
² commissione: ora, siccome il recente

on our prices, we find it impossible to purchase the remainder, and, indeed³, think ourselves fortunate in having secured the parcels alluded to⁴ in our last. We feel pleasure in the reflection, that the change which must consequently take place⁵ in your market will enable you⁶ to profit considerably by this shipment⁷, and induce you to favour us again with your orders.

The invoice amount £... is pleaced⁸ to your debit, and our drafts on Hamburgh of this day balance⁹ the sum. The bill of lading we have sent to Bremen, and the order for insurance to Amsterdam, both by this post.

We are, &c.

P. S. We beg¹⁰ to inform you, that the ship has already cleared outwards at the Custom-house¹¹.

³ veramente
⁴ d'aver assicurate le partite accennate
⁵ aver luogo
⁶ vi porrà in grado
⁷ spedizione

⁸ posto
⁹ pareggiano
¹⁰ ci facciamo un dovere
¹¹ ha già adempiuto la formalità della Dogana ed è libero di partire.

To Bremen.

London.

Sir,

Enclosed we have the honour to hand you bill of lading and invoice, of sundry¹ articles, specified at foot, which we have shipped on board the neutral vessel the Latona. Captain, P. for account and risk of our mutual friends, Messrs. J. Y. and Co. of Lubec. We refer you² to the said gentlemen for directions as to their disposal³, and are, with esteem, &c.

¹ vari
² rivolgetevi
³ per le ulteriori istruzioni riguardo alla disposizione del medesimi.

To London.

Bremen.

Since my last of the..., the Latona arrived safely[1], and the goods landed[2]; I am, however, sorry[3] to inform you that there is a deficiency[4] of ninety pounds in the weight of the coffee, which Captain P. refuses to indemnify[5] having written in the bill of lading, "weight and contents unknown[6];" besides this, the unshattered[7] state of the casks[8] justifies his refusal, as it clears him[9] from any imputation of embezzlement[10].

It is my duty[11] to inform you as shipper[12], of this accident, and I also think it right[13] to accompany my assertion by the enclosed sworn certificate of the weighers at our town hall[14], which I hope will enable you[15] to recover the deficiency from the sellers, as[16] our friends may impute this to my negligence. I send them, to night, a full statement[17] of the circumstance, and am, &c.

[1] felicemente
[2] furono sbarcate
[3] peraltro dispiacente
[4] calo
[5] indennizzare, rifare il danno
[6] contenuto ignoto
[7] perfetto
[8] barili
[9] giacchè lo assolve
[10] infedeltà
[11] dovere
[12] caricatore
[13] giudico pure opportuno
[14] accluso certificato giurato dai nostri pesatori pubblici
[15] vi porrà in grado
[16] giacchè
[17] questa sera un pieno ragguaglio.

To London.

Embden.

As we are willing to accept your proposal of settling our dispute by[1] arbitration, we have, to this end sent copies of all the papers relative to the transaction[2] to

[1] di comporre la nostra differenza per
[2] affare

our friend Mr. H., whom we have empowered³ to act and decide for us. He will communicate to you our intentions, which we fully confirm.

³ dato facolta.

To Mr. P. Hamburgh.

Copenhagen.

We have herewith¹ the honour to inform you, that your kind² commission has been executed with all the promptitude and attention it was capable of³. We are fully convinced that you will find the several sorts of coffee corresponding to your wishes. Notwithstanding the differrence there is in the prices in the respective markets, according to the invoice⁴ which accompanies the present, the amount is four thousand dollars, or, in Hamburgh money, nine thousand two hundred and sixty marcs banco, for which we have debited your account. We hope, however, you will have no objection to our drawing⁵ the principal part, which⁶ we have done, to the amount of nine thousand marcs banco, in four bills⁷ of the same sum each, drawn for⁸ this day, all to the order of B. R. and Co.; the balance we'll let remain till your next kind orders⁹.

The coffee (both in hogsheads and bags¹⁰, as mentioned in the invoice) will be shipped¹¹ to morrow, per¹² the Harmonia, Captain Oles, who sails at farthest¹³, in eight days. We have judged it prudent to make out¹⁴

1 colla presente
2 ben accetta
3 di cui era suscettibile
4 conformemente alla fattura
5 ci permetterete di trattare
6 il che
7 cambiali
8 tratte
9 lasceremo il saldo sino ai prossimi vostri graditi ordini
10 tanto in botti che in sacchi
11 caricato
12 sul
13 che partirà al più tardi
14 stendere

two bills of lading, one for the hogsheads, and another for the bags, both of which you will find enclosed, Recommending ourselves to your friendship,
We are, &c.

To London.

Amsterdam.

I duly received your favour of the 10th inst. and beg a continuance of[1] your mercantile advices, being willing to embrace every opportunity of enlivening[2] our correspondence. I am not in the habit of making[3] considerable speculations, but still[4] have a very extensive regular trade, which employs yearly a large proportion[5] of my capital, and, I am happy to say, has invariably prospered[6].

I have been accustomed to address my orders to an eminent house in your city, whose negligence however in retarding the shipment[7] of some articles occasioned me lately a very considerable loss.

Despatch[8] and attention are primary qualities in[9] a merchant or agent.

Encouraged by the testimony of my friends B. and Co. in your favour, I am inclined[10] to make a trial by giving you[11] an order, in the execution of which I recommend despatch.

In a fortnight[12], I find by the public prints[13], there will

[1] e vi prego di continuare a trasmettermi
[2] di ravvivare
[3] non è mia consuetudine di fare
[4] ma pure
[5] parte
[6] ha progredito sempre vantaggiosamente
[7] il cui indugio nella spedizione
[8] sollecitudine
[9] sono qualità essenziali in
[10] incoraggiato dalla favorevole opinione emessa a vostro riguardo dai miei amici B. e Comp. sono disposto
[11] una prova col darvi
[12] fra quindici giorni
[13] pubblici fogli che

be a sale of cotton, at which I beg you to purchase for my account: —

Ten bales of Smyrna, eight bales of Georgia, and twelve bales of Demerara; in all, thirty bales of cotton. The probable prices of the different qualities I note at foot[14], without absolutely limiting you to them, leaving this to your own judgment. I merely remark that[15], from the tenor of my various advices. I think the prices likely to run at these rates[16]. The invoice I wish to have as soon as possible, in order to effect insurance, which I prefer doing in Amsterdam; because, being on the spot, I am acquainted with[17] the solidity of the underwriters[18]. It is moreover[19] my opinion, that the English underwriters are by much too captious[20] not sufficiently under control[21], and keep their clients too long out of their money[22], which certainly is a very great inconvenience, and severely felt by some houses, in cases of total losses by ships. You may value on me for the amount of my order, at 2½ usances[23]; and, trusting to your exertions[24] for my interest,

I remain, &c.

[14] Il segno in calce
[15] vi faccio semplicemente osservare che
[16] suppongo che tali saranno all'incirca i prezzi
[17] sul luogo, conosco
[18] assicuratori

[19] Inoltre —
[20] cavillosi
[21] sorveglianza
[22] protraggono troppo a lungo il risarcimento spettante al loro assicurati
[23] due mesi e mezzo
[24] confidando nella vostra premura·

Commendatizia e creditoria.[1]

Stuttgart, li . . . .

La presente vi sarà consegnata dal Signor Carlo Mayer jr. che vi raccomandiamo di una maniera tutta particolare.[2]

[1] letter of introduction and credit   [2] whom we recommend to your kindness.

— 174 —

Quanto ai danari che il Signor Mayer potrebbe abbisognare, noi l'accreditiamo presso di voi fino alla concorrenza della somma di 1000 sc. pr. crt.[*] (diciamo mille scudi pruss. crt.) che vi compiacerete pagargli per nostro conto verso le sue tratte su Francoforte s[M. inviandoci una delle sue quitanze.

Aggradite unitamente ai nostri ringraziamenti per le cortesie che userete al nostro raccomandato le protestazioni della distinta stima, colla quale abbiamo l'onore di essere

N. N. e Co.

Valevole per 6 mesi dal di d'oggi[3]

[3] Curency   [4] valid for six months.

Signori N. N. in Amburgo.

Ci rechiamo a dovere[1] il notificarvi, che il signor Martino Burmester, bramando di rinunziare agli affari, di qui innanzi si ritira dalla nostra casa, che per trent'anni si onorevolmente rappresentò. Comechè questo suo ritiro ad un vivere più tranquillo ed agiato nella sua villa vicinissima a questa città ci arrechi il rincrescimento di vederci privi della sua intelligente cooperazione,[2] è d'uopo però dire che la sua vita laboriosa meritava questa ricreazione, di che ci rallegriamo con lui. Ciò non di meno nulla sarà mutato nel corso de' nostri affari,[3] poichè il sig. Martino Burmester si fa sostituire[4] dal degno suo figlio Roberto, il quale col giorno d'oggi entra qual socio nel nostro negozio.

[1] we take the liberty
[2] awakens our deep regret at being deprived of his intelligent cooperation
[3] in the routine of our business   [4] offers as his successor

Portiamo speranza che neppur voi, Signori, cangerete per nulla le nostre antiche relazioni d'affari¹ con reciproca² soddisfazione condotti, che anzi ci conserverete sempre quella fiducia, di cui ci studieremo con ogni cura essere meritevoli.

¹ business-connexion   ² mutual.

Signore!

Facendo io quind'innanzi¹ in questa città le veci della casa Amsie e Rose, che sta per cessare, prego gli antichi amici d'appoggiarmi le loro commissioni di compre e vendite, assicurandoli, che verranno con pari zelo eseguite,² come da 50 anni in qua nella nostra casa si soleva. Favorite di esaminare³ il compiegato listino dei prezzi e quello della borsa, e gradite le assicurazioni di perfetta stima, onde sono

obbediente servitore
GIACOMO AMSLER.

¹ henceforward   ² attended to
³ allow me to request your attention.

FINE DELLA SECONDA PARTE

APPENDICE

Quest'appendice, composta di brani di ottimi autori, deve servire non solo a rendere famigliare il loro stile per comprenderli più facilmente, ma ben anco per acquistare uno stile elegante e veramente inglese; a questo scopo è necessario che l'allievo dopo aver tradotto un brano in italiano lo ritraduca in inglese, in iscritto se studia da sè, a voce se studia col maestro. Epperciò io non ho messo in questa appendice alcun brano italiano da tradursi in inglese; quando l'allievo ha fatto un numero sufficiente di temi per apprendere bene le regole e farsi un tesoro di parole e frasi, non deve far altro che composizioni o traduzioni dalla lingua straniera nella propria; il tradurre dall'italiano in inglese non serve che ad abbituarci a scrivere e parlare parole inglesi in stile italiano.

THE PHILOSOPHER OUTDONE.

A learned philosopher being very busy[1] in his study, a little girl came to ask him for some fire. "But," says the doctor, "you have nothing to take it in;" and as he was going to fetch[2] something for that purpose, the little girl stooped down at the fire-place, and taking some cold ashes[3] in one hand, she put burning embers[4] on them with the other. The astonished doctor threw down his books, saying. "With all my learning, I should never have found out that expedient".

[1] affaccendato
[2] prendere
[3] cenere
[4] bragia.

Dean Swift advice respecting Servants.

" If you want a servant, take one; if you wish to be badly served, take two; if you wish to serve yourself, take three; If you wish to be well served, serve yourself."

A Golden Rule.

Industry will make a man a purse and frugality will find him strings¹ for it. Neither the purse nor the strings will cost him any thing. He who has it, should only draw the strings as frugality directs, and he will be sure always to find a useful penny at the bottom of it.² The servants of industry are known by their livery; it is always *whole* and *wholesome*. Idleness travles very leisurely and poverty soon overtakes³ him. Look at the *ragged*⁴ *slaves* of *Idleness*, and judge which is the best master to serve *Industry* or *Idleness?*

¹ cordicella   ³ ragglungere
² In fondo   ⁴ cienclogo.

How to become Learned.

The celebrated John Locke was asked how he had contrived to accumulate a mine of knowledge so rich, yet so extensive and deep. He replied, that he attributed what little he knew to the not having been ashamed to ask for information; and to the rule he had laid down of conversing with all descriptions of men, on those topics chiefly that formed their own peculiar professions and pursuits.

Dr. Watts.

It was so natural for Dr. Watts, when a child, to speak in rhyme, that even at the very time he wished

to avoid it, he could not. His father was displeased at this propensity, and threatened to whip¹ him, if he did not leave off² making verses. One day, when he was about to put his threat in execution, the child burst out into tears, and on his knees said:
"Pray, father, do some pity take,
And I will no more verses make."

¹ sforzare   ² cessare.

ABSTRACTION.

Sir Isaac Newton, finding himself extremely cold one winter evening, drew his chair very close to the grate,¹ in which a large fire had recently been lighted. By degrees the fire having completely kindled,² Sir Isaac felt the heat intolerably intense, and rung his bell with unusual violence. His servant was not at hand at the moment, but he soon made his appearance. By this time, Sir Isaac was almost litterally roasted. "Remove the grate, you lazy rascal!" he exclaimed, in a tone of irritation very uncommon with that amiable and bland philosopher; "remove the grate before I am burnt to death!" "And pray Master," said the servant, "might you not rather draw back your chair?" "Upon my word," said Sir Isaac, smiling, "I never thought of that."

¹ griglia   ² acceso.

THE MOST UNHAPPY.

Cosroes, King of Persia, in conversation with two philosopher and his vizir, asked — "What situation of man is most to be deplored?" One of the philosophers maintained, that it was old age accompanied with extreme poverty; the other, that it was to have the body oppressed by infirmities, the mind worn out, and the heart broken by a heavy series of misfortunes. "I know a condition more to be pitied," said the Vizir, "and it is that of him, who has passed through life without doing good; and who, unexpectedly is surprised by death.

KNOWLEDGE AND IGNORANCE.

The man of knowledge lives eternally after his death, while his members are reduced to dust beneath[1] the tomb. But the ignorant man is dead, even while he walks upon the earth: he is numbered with living men, and yet he existeth[1] not.

Arabian Author.

[1] sotto   [2] nella poesia e prosa poetica la terza persona singolare riceve talvolta *th* invèce di *s*.

TASTE AND KNOWLDGE.

Taste, like an artificial[1] canal, winds[2] through a beautiful country, but its borders[3] are confined and its term limited. Knowledge navigates the ocean and is perpetually on voyages of discovery.

[1] gusto   [2] gira   [3] orlo.

MUSICAL TASTE.

The ass has been frequently made one of the parties in the most popular fables from Aesop downwards[1]. The following is not much known. A trial[2] of skill in singing being agreed upon between the cuckoo and the nightingale, the ass was chosen as umpire[3]. After each had done his best, the sagacious animal declared that the nightingale sang extremely well; but for a good plain song the cuckoo was far his superior, — How many such critics there are in the world!

[1] in poi   [2] scommessa, cimento   [3] arbitro.

Political Prudence.

Wise men say nothing in dangerous times. The lion called the sheep, and asked her if his breath smelt; she said " Ay ", and he bit off her head for a fool. He called the wolf, and asked him. He said " No," and he tore him in pieces for a flatterer. At last he called for the fox, and asked him. " Truly," said Reynard, " I have got a cold, and cannot smell."

Devouring Books.

It is recorded of Madame de Stael Holstein, that before she was fifteen years of age she had "*devoured*" 600 novels in three months, so that she must have read more than six a-day upon an average[1]. Louis XVI., during the five months and seven days of his imprisonment immediately preceding his death, read 157 volumes, or one a-day. If this species of gluttony is pardonable in circumstances like those of Louis, it is less so in those of a young lady of fourteen or fifteen. No one can have time for reflection who reads at this rapid rate, and, whatever may be thought, these *devourers* of books are guilty[2] of abusing nature to an extent[3] as much greater than those who overcharge their stomachs, as the intellectual powers are higher than the animal propensities. Thousands of young people spend their time in perpetual reading, or rather in *devouring* books. It is true, the food is light; but it occupies the mental faculties for the time in fruitless efforts, and operates[4] to exclude food of a better quality.

Annals of Education.

[1] in media
[2] colpevole
[3] estensione, portata
[4] produce l'effetto

VIRTUE MAN'S TRUE INTEREST.

I find myself existing upon a little spot,[1] surrounded every where by an immense unknown expansion. Where am I? What sort of place do I inhabit? Is it exactly accommodated, in every instance[2], to my convenience? Is there no excess of cold, none of heat, to offend me? Am I never annoyed by animals either of my own or of a different kind? Is every thing subservient to me, as though I had ordered all myself? — No — nothing like it — the furthest from it possible. — The world appears not, then, originally made for the private convenience of me alone.

But is it not possible, so to accommodate it by my own particular industry? If to accomodate man and beast, heaven and earth, be beyond me, it is not possible. — What consequence then follows? or can there be any other than this: If I seek an interest of my own, detached[3] from that of others, I seek an interest which is chimerical, and can never have existed?

How then must I determine? Have I no interest at all? — If I have not, I am a fool for staying here. It is a smoky house:.and the sooner I am out of it the better, — But why no interest? — Can I be contented with none, but one separate and detached? — Is a social interest, joined with others, such an absurdity as not to be admitted? — The bee,[4] the beaver,[5] and the tribes of herding[6] animals, are enow to convince me, that the thing is somewhere at least possible. How, then, am I assured that it is not ebually true of man? — Admit it; and what follows? If so, then honour and justice are my interest: then the whole train of moral virtues are my

[1] spazio, sito
[2] in ogni riguardo
[3] staccato
[4] l'ape
[5] castoro
[6] armenti

interest; without some portion of which not even thieves can maintain society.

But, further still — I stop not here — I pursue this social interest as far as I can trace my several relations, I pass from my own stock, my own neighbourhood, my own nation, to the whole race of mankind, as dispersed throughout the earth. — Am I not related to them all by the mutual aids of commerce, by the general intercourse² of arts and letters, by that common nature of which we all participate?

Again — I must have food and clothing — Without a proper genial warmth, I instantly perish — Am I not related, in this view, to the very earth itself? to the distant sun, from whose beams³ I derive vigour? to that stupendous course and order of the infinite host of heaven, by which the times and seasons ever uniformly pass on? — Were this order once confounded, I could not probably survive a moment; so absolutely do I depend on this common general welfare. —

(Harris.)

² commercio   ³ raggi.

THE GIANT¹ AND THE DWARF²

Once upon a time a giant and a dwarf were friends, and kept together.³ They made a bargain that they never would forsake each other, but go seek adventures. The first battle they fought was with two Saracens; and the dwarf who was very courageous, dealt⁴ one of the champions a most angry blow. It did the Saracen but very little injury, who lifting up his sword, fairly struck off the poor dwarf's arm. He was now in a woful plight⁵

¹ gigante   ⁴ menò
² nano   ⁵ pietoso stato
³ vivevano assieme

but the giant coming to his assistance, in a short time left the two dead man's head out of spite.

They then travelled on to another adventure. This was against three blood-minded[4] Satyrs, who were carrying away a damsel in distress. The dwarf was not quite so fierce now as before, but for all that[7], struck the first blow, which was returned by another, that knocked out his eye; but the giant was soon up with them, and, had they not fled, would certainly have killed them every one. They were all very joyful for this victory, and the damsel who was relieved fell in love with the giant, and married him.

They now travelled far, and farther than I can tell, till they met with a company of robbers. The giant, for the first time, was foremost now, but the dwarf was not far behind. The battle was stout[8] and long. Wherever the giant came, all fell before him; but the dwarf had like to have been killed more than once. At last the victory declared for the two adventurers; but the dwarf lost his leg. The dwarf had now lost an arm, a leg, and an eye, while the giant was without a single wound. Upon which he cried out to his little companion: "My little hero, this is glorious sport; let us get one victory more, and then we shall have honour for ever."—"No", cries the dwarf, who by this time was grown wiser, "no, I declare off[9]; I'll fight no more: for I find in every battle, that you get all the honour and rewards, but all the blows fall upon me."

Goldsmith.

[4] sanguinarj
[7] nondimeno
[8] ostinata, fiera
[9] me la cavo.

HOW TO COMUNICATE BAD NEWS

Scene: The room of Mr. Gr., at Oxford.

(Enter to him his father's steward).

Mr. G. Ha Jervas, how are you, my old boy? How do things go on at home?
Steward. Bad enough, your Honour, the magpie¹'s dead.
Mr. G. Poor Mag²! So he is gone. How came he to die?
Steward. Over-ate himself,³ Sir.
Mr. G. Did he, faith! A greed dog⁴! Why, what did he get, that he liked so well?
Steward. Horse-flesh,⁵ Sir! He died of eating horse-flesh.
Mr. G. How came he to get so much horse-flesh?
Steward. All your father's horses, Sir.
Mr. G. What, are they dead too?
Steward. Aye, Sir, they died of overwork.⁶
Mr. G. And why were they overworked, pray?
Steward. To carry water, Sir.
Mr. G. To carry water? And what were they carrying water for?
Steward. Sure, Sir, to put out the fire.
Mr. G. Fire! What fire?
Steward. Oh, Sir, your father's house is burnt down to the ground.
Mr. G. My father's house burnt down! And how came it set on fire?
Steward. I think, Sir, it must have been the torches.⁷
Mr. G. Torches! What torches?
Steward. At you mother's funeral.

¹ gazza
² abb. di Magpie
³ mangiò troppo
⁴ ingorda bestia
⁵ carne di cavallo
⁶ dal troppo lavoro
⁷ le fiaccole

Mr. G. My mother dead!

Steward. Ah, poor lady! She never looked up⁸ after it.

Mr. G. After what?

Steward. The loss of your father.

Mr. G. My father gone too!

Steward. Yes, poor gentleman! He took to his bed as soon as he heard of it.

Mr. G. Heard of what?

Steward. The bad news, Sir, an⁹ please your Honour.

Mr. G. What, more miseries! More bad news!

Steward. Yes, Sir, your bank has failed, and you are not worth a shilling in the world. I made bold [10], Sir, to come to wait on you to tell you about it, for I thought, you would like to hear the news.

⁸ si rimise   ⁹ se   [10] mi feci ardito.

AN INHERITANCE.

A. Ah, Sir, you will be very much afflicted. I have most lamentable tidings¹ to communicate to you.

B. What is it? Can one of my creditors have presumed to threaten me?

A. Not that. The misfortune, that I have to announce to you, is far greater. Our heavenly Father.... alas, we are all mortal! do not be terrified²

B. What's the meaning of your miserable whining and sighing³.

A. Your uncle has been stuck with an apoplectic fit⁴,

B. How, my uncle is dead?

¹ notizie   ³ lamenti e sospiri
² non vi spaventate   ⁴ colpo apopletico

A. He has only just given up the ghost⁵; he expired in my arms.
B. What a lamentable event!
A. He loved you much, as it appears. An hour before his death he was still speaking of you.
B. Ah, the good venerable man, the excellent pious man! He has probably appointed me his universal legatee⁶! — But tell me, is he, indeed, dead?
A. I have received his last sigh; I have closed his eyes.
B. May God have him in his holy keeping⁷! it is well for him! let us not envey him his repose. Do you think he has left a handsome property?
A. His strong-box⁸ is piled up high with money-bags.
B. Oh cruel fate! thou snatchest from me him whom I held dearest upon earth. I shall never be consoled for this loss; throughout my whole life I shall bewail the untimely demise⁹ of my dear late uncle. He was the most deserving, the most virtuous of men; ah, woe is me¹⁰!
A. I know, he was worth more than a hundred thousand pounds.
B. Go quick, and make the necessary preparations for the interment. Let the large hearse¹¹ with six horses be kept in readiness. I wish the funeral obsequies to take place with all imaginable pomp, over his grave a marble-monument shall be erected with a magnificent epitaph, that may hand down¹² to posterity the excellent qualities of my dear uncle. The whole house from the top to the bottom¹³ shall be hung with black: Every one shall put on crape and mourning,¹⁴ and the whole town

⁵ ha reso l'anima
⁶ leg itario universale
⁷ santa custodia
⁸ scrigno
⁹ morte immatura
¹⁰ me disgraziato
¹¹ carro funebre
¹² tramandare
¹³ da cima a fondo
¹⁴ velo e lutto

shall be invited, to pay the last honours to the defunct.

A. By the bye, I had nearly forgotten it; I found these papers in his pocket, and laid hold of them lest they might fall into strange hands; perhaps you will find some notices of his past life in them, which will surprise you.

B. Let us see! Hum, doctors'bills, apothecaries'bills! a list of his debts! it is very considerable. — Hah, here comes the chief thing: the will. Let us read it: "I bequeath to God my poor soul." — Good ! — "I bequeath to my neighbour N. for the friendship which he has constantly had for me, my house, goods and chattels[13]; to my coachman my carriage and horses; to my manservant my whole wardrobe etc."

A. But you, Sir, should he have forgotten you?

B. Strange! I see here a quantity of legacies, and my name not amongst them. — But here it comes. "As for my nephew, who has never shown me the slightest affection, who is a spendthrift[14], a low libertine...." — Oh, the old dotard !

A. Read further, Sir!

B. "And who would never hearken[17] to my good counsel, I ought to entirely disinherit him...." ·What malignancy! — "Yet, as he most probably has not a farthing in the world, I give him voluntarily one shilling, that he may be enabled to pay hangman's fee[18]. He may content himself with that!"

A. How many mourning coaches shall I bespeak for the funeral procession, Sir?

B. Pack yourself off,[20] Sirrah[21] !

[13] beni mobili
[14] prodigo
[17] ascoltare
[16] pagar le spese del boia
[19] ordinare
[20] vattene al diavolo
[21] birbone.

Mary Queen of Scots.

To all the charms of beauty, and the utmost[1] elegance of external form, Mary adding those accomplishments which render their impressions irresistible, was polite, affable, insinuating sprightly[2] and capable of speaking and writing with equal ease[3] and dignity; sudden, however, and violent in all her attachments, because her heart was warm and unsuspicious,[4] impatient of contradiction, because she had been accustomed from her infancy to be treated as a queen; no stranger[5] on some occasions, to dissimulation, which, in that perfidious court where she received her education, was reckoned[6] among the necessary arts of government; not insensible to flattery, or unconscious of that pleasure with which almost every woman beholds[7] the influence of her own beauty. Formed with the qualities that we love, not with the talents that we admire, she was an agreeable woman, rather than an illustrious queen. The vivacity of her spirit, not sufficiently tempered with sound judgment[8] and the warmth of her heart, which was not at all times under the restraint[9] of discretion, betrayed[10] her both into errors and crimes. To say that she was most unfortunate, will not account[11] for that long and almost uninterrupted succession of calamities which befell her; we must likewise add, that she was often imprudent. Her passion for Darnely was rash[12] youthful, and excessive. And though the sudden transition to the opposite extreme was the natural effect of her illrequi-

[1] massima
[2] gaia
[3] facilità
[4] fiducioso
[5] aliena
[6] stimato
[7] mira
[8] retto giudizio
[9] controllo
[10] trassero
[11] non basterebbe
[12] impetuoso

ted[13] love, and of his ingratitude, insolence, and brutality; yet neither these, nor Bothwell's artful address and important services can justify her attachment to that nobleman. Even the manners of the age, licentious as they were, are no apology[14] for this unhappy passion; nor can they induce us to look on that tragical and infamous scene (the murder of her husband Darnley) which followed upon it, with less abhorrence. Humanity will draw a veil over this part of her character, which it cannot approve, and may, perhaps, prompt[15] some to impute her actions to her situation, more than to her disposition; and to lament the unhappiness of the former rather than accuse the perverseness of the latter, Mary's sufferings[16] exceed both in degree and duration, those tragical distresses which the fancy has feigned to excite sorrow and commiseration; and while we survey[17] them, we are apt altogether[18] to forget her frailties; we think of her faults with less indignation, and approve of our tears, as if they were shed for a person who had attained much nearer to pure virtue.

With regard to the queen's person, a circumstance not to be omitted in writing the history of a female reign, all contemporary authors agree in ascribing to Mary the utmost beauty of countenance[19] and elegance of shape[20] of which the human form is capable. Her hair was black; though, according to the fashion of the age she frequently wore borrowed[21] locks,[21] and of different colours. Her eyes were a dark grey, her complexion[23] was exquisitely fine and her hands and arms remarkably delicate, both as to shape and colour. Her stature

[13] mal contracambiato
[14] scusa
[15] suggerir
[16] soffereuze
[17] considerare
[18] del tutto
[19] faccia
[20] forma
[21] prestati, finti
[22] ricci
[23] tinta

was of a height¹⁴ that rose to the majestic. She danced, walked, and rode with equal grace. Her taste for music was just, and she sang and played on the lute with uncommon skill. Towards the end of her life she began to grow fat: and her long confinement, and the coldness of the house in which she was imprisoned brought on a rheumatism, which deprived¹⁵ her of her limbs¹⁶ "No man," says Brantome, "ever beheld¹⁷ her person without admiration and love, or will read her history without sorrow."

Robertson.

¹⁴ altezza
¹⁵ privarono
¹⁶ membra
¹⁷ mirò.

THE STORY OF A DISABLED SOLDIER.

I was born in Shropshire; my father was a labourer, and died when I was five years old: so I was put upon the parish. As he had been a wandering sort of a man,¹ the parishioners were not able to tell to what parish I belonged, or where I was born; so they sent me to another parish, and that parish sent me to a third. I thought in my heart, they kept sending me about so long, that they would not let me be born in any parish at all; but at last, however, they fixed me. I had some disposition to be a scholar,² and was resolved at least to know my letters; but the master of the work-house put me to business as soon as I was able to handle a mallet;³ and here I lived an easy kind of life for five years. I only wrought ten hours in the day, and had my meat and drink provided for my labour. It is true, I was not suffered to stir out⁴ of the house, for fear, as they said, I should run away; but what of that, I

¹ girovago
² letterato
³ maneggiare il maglietto
⁴ far un passo fuori

had the liberty of the whole house, and the yard before the door; and that was enough for me. I was then bound out to a farmer, where I was up both early and late: but I ate and drank well, and liked my business well enough, till he died, when I was obliged to provide for myself; so I was resolved to go seek my fortune.

In this manner, I went from town to town, worked when I could get employment, and starved when I could get none: when happening one day to go through a field belonging to a Justice of peace, I spied a hare⁵ crossing the path just before me, and I believe the devil put it in my head to fling my stick at it; — Well, what will you have on't? I killed the hare, and was bringing it away, when the Justice himself met me: he called me a poacher⁷ and a villain, and collaring me, desired I would give an account of myself. I fell upon my knees, begged his worship's pardon, and began to give a full account of all that I knew of my breed, seed, and generation; but though I gave a very true account, the Justice said I could give no account; so I was indicted at sessions, found guilty of being poor, and sent up to London to Newgate, in order to be transported as a vagabond.

People may say this and that of being in jail, but for my part, I found Newgate as agreeable a place as ever I was in in all my life. I had my bellyful⁸ to eat and drink, and did no work at all. This kind of life was too good to last for ever, so I was taken out of prison after five months, put on board a ship, and sent off with two hundred more to the plantations. We had but an indifferent passage, for being all confined in the hold,⁹ more than a hundred of our people died for want of sweet air, and those that remained were sickly enough, God

⁵ scoral una lepre
⁶ gli scaglini il mio bastone
⁷ cacciator clandestino
⁸ corpacciata (pieno il corpo)
⁹ confiscati nella stiva

knows. When we came ashore, we were sold to the planters, and I was bound for seven years more. As I was no scholar, for I did not know my letters, I was obliged to work among the negroes; and I served out my time, as in duty bound to do.

When my time was expired, I worked my passage home, and glad I was to see old England again, because I loved my country. I was afraid, however, that I should be indicted for a vagabond once more, so I did not much care to go down into the country, but kept about the town, and did little jobs [10] when I could get them.

I was very happy in this manner, for some time; till one evening, coming home from work, two men knocked me down, and then desired me to stand. They belonged to a press-gang. I was carried before the Justice, and as I could give no account of myself, I had my choice left, whether to go on board a man of war, or list for a soldier. I chose the latter; and in this post of a gentleman, I served two campaigns in Flanders, was at the battles of Val and Fontenoy, and received but one wound, through the breast here; but the doctor of our regiment soon made me well again.

When the peace came on, I was discharged; [11] and as I could not work, because my wound was sometimes troublesome, I listed for a landsman in the East-India Company's service. I have fought the French in three pitched [12] battles; and I verily believe, that, if I could read or write, our captain would have made me a corporal. But it was not my good fortune to have any promotion, for I soon fell sick, and so got leave to return home again with forty pounds in my pocket. This was at the beginning of the present war, and I hoped to be set on shore, and to have the pleasure of spending my money;

[10] lavori   [11] ful congedato   [12] campali

but the government wanted men, and so I was pressed for a sailor, before ever I could set foot ou shore.

The boatswain[13] found me, as he said, an obstinate fellow: he swore he knew I understood my business well, but that I shammed[14] Abraham, to be idle; but, God knows, I knew nothing of sea-business; and he beat me, without considering what he was about. I had still, however, my forty pounds, and that was some comfort to me under every beating; and the money I might have had to this day, but that our ship was taken by the French, and so I lost all.

Our crew[15] was carried into Brest, and many of them died, because they were not used to live in a jail; but for my part, it was nothing to me, for I was seasoned. One night, as I was asleep on the bed of boards,[16] with a warm blanket[17] about me, for I always loved to lie well, I was awakened by the boatswain, who had a dark lantern, in his hand. "Jack," said he to me, "will you knock out the French sentry's[18] brains?" "I don't care," says I, striving to keep myself awake. "if I lend a hand." "Then follow me," said he, "and I hope we shall do business." So up I got, and though we had no arms, we went down to the door, where both sentries were posted, and rushing upon them, seized their arms in a moment, and knocked them down. From thence, nine of us ran together to the quay, and seizing the first boat we met, got out of the harbour, and put to sea. We had not been here three days before we were taken up by the *Dorset* privateer, who were glad of so many good hands, and we consented to run our chance. However, we had not so much luck as we expected. In three days we fell in with the *Pompadour* privateer, of forty guns,

[13] nostromo
[14] fingere
[15] ciurma
[16] asse
[17] coperta di lana
[18] sentinella

while we had but twenty-three; so to it we went, yard-arm and yard-arm. The fight lasted for three hours, and I verily believe we should have taken the Frenchman, had we but had some more men left behind; but, unfortunately, we lost all our men just as we were going to get the victory.

I was once more in the power of the French, and I believe it would have gone hard with me, had I been brought back to Brest; but, by good fortune, we were retaken by the *Viper*. I had almost forgot to tell you, that in this engagement I was wounded in two places: I lost four fingers of the left hand, and my leg was shot off. If I had had the good fortune to have lost my leg and use of my hand on board a king's ship, and not on board a privateer, I should have been entitled to clothing and maintenance during the rest of my life; but that was not my chance: one man is born with a silver spoon in his mouth, and another with a wooden ladle."
However, blessed be God, I enjoy good health, and will for ever love liberty and old England. Liberty, property, and old England, for ever, huzza !

— Thus saying, he limped off,¹⁹ leaving me in admiration at his intrepidity and content; nor could I avoid acknowledging, that an habitual acquaintance with misery serves better than philosophy to teach us to despise it.

(*Goldsmith.*)

¹⁸ ramaiuolo ¹⁹ se ne andò zoppicando.

ON LYING.

I really know nothing more criminal, more mean, and more ridiculous, than lying. It is the production either of malice, cowardice, or vanity; and generally

¹ manca il suo scopo

misses its aim in every one of these views, for lies are always detected, sooner or later. If I tell a malicious lie, in order to affect any man's fortune or character, I may indeed injure him for some time; but I shall be sure to be the greatest sufferer at last; for as soon as I am detected² (and detected I most certainly shall be). I am blasted³ for the infamous attempt, and whatever is said afterwards to the disadvantage of that person, however true, passes for calumny. If I lie, or equivocate (for it is the same thing), in order to excuse myself for something I have said or done, and to avoid the danger or the shame that I apprehend from it, I discover at once my fear as well as my falsehood; and only increase, instead of avoiding the danger and the shame; I show myself to be the lowest and meanest of mankind, and am sure to be always treated as such. Fear, instead of avoiding, invites danger; for concealed cowards⁵ will insult known ones. If one has had the misfortune to be in the wrong, there is something noble in frankly owning⁶ it; it is the only way of atoning⁷ for it, and the only way of being forgiven. Equivocating, evading,⁸ in order to remove a present danger or inconvenience, is something so mean, and betrays⁹ so much fear, that whoever practises them always deserves to be, and often will be kicked¹⁰. There is another sort of lies, inoffensive enough in themselves, but wonderfully ridiculous: I mean those lies which a mistaken vanity suggests, that defeat the very end for which they are calculated, and terminate in the humiliation and confusion of their author, who is sure to be detected. These are chiefly narrative and historical lies, all intended to do infinite honour to their

² scoperto
³ to blast, distruggere la ripu'a-
zione
⁴ aumento
⁵ vigliacchi
⁶ confessare
⁷ espiare
⁸ confondere
⁹ dimostra
¹⁰ scacciato a calci

author. He is always the hero of his own romances; he has been in dangers, from which nobody but himself ever escaped; he has seen with his own eyes whatever other people have heard or read of; and has ridden more miles post In one day, than ever courier went in two. He is soon discovered, and as soon becomes the object of universal contempt and ridicule. Remember then, as long as you live, that nothing but strict truth can carry you through the world, with either your conscience or your honour unwounded It is not only your duty, but your interest: as a proof of which, you may always observe that the greatest fools are the greatest liars. For my own part, I judge by every man's truth, of his degree of understanding[11].

(Chesterfield).

[11] intelligenza.

CHARACTER OF ALFRED.

The merit of this prince, both in private and public life, may with advantage be set in opposition to that of any monarch or citizen which the annals of any age or any nation can present to us. He seems indeed to be the complete model of that perfect character, which, under the denomination of a sage or wise man, the philosophers have been fond of delineating, rather as a fiction of their imagination than in hopes of ever seeing it reduced to practice: so happily were all his virtues tempered together, so justly were they blended[1], and so powerfully did each prevent the other from exceeding its proper bounds[2]. He knew how to conciliate the most enterprising spirit with the coolest[3] moderation, the most

[1] contemperate, commiste, equilibrate
[2] limiti, confini
[3] più giudiziosa, più fredda

obstinate perseverance with the easiest flexibility; the most severe justice with the greatest lenity; the greatest rigour in command with the greatest affability of deportment; the highest capacity and inclination for science, with the most shining⁴ talents for action. His civil and his military virtues are almost equally the objects of our admiration, excepting only, that the former being more rare among princes, as well as more useful seem chiefly⁵ to challenge⁶ our applause. Nature also, as if desirous that so bright⁷ a production of her skill⁸ should be set in the fairest light⁹, had bestowed on him all bodily¹⁰ accomplishments, vigour of limbs¹¹, dignity of shape¹² and air, and a pleasant, engaging¹³. and open countenance¹⁴. Fortune alone, by throwing¹⁵ him into that barbarous age, deprived him of historians worthy¹⁶ to transmit his fame to posterity; and we wish to see him delineated in more lively colours, and with more particular strokes¹⁷ that we may at least perceive some of those small specks and blemishes¹⁸, from which, as a man, it is impossible he could be entirely exempted.

Hume.

⁴ brillanti
⁵ principalmente, in specie
⁶ (sfidare) provocare
⁷ brillante, stupenda
⁸ perizia, abilità
⁹ venisse collocata nella luce più propizia
¹⁰ di corpo, corporale
¹¹ membra
¹² forma, figura
¹³ interessante, attraente, simpatico
¹⁴ viso, volto
¹⁵ gettare
¹⁶ degni
¹⁷ tratti di pennello
¹⁸ macchie e difetti.

ADVICE TO A YOUNG TRADESMAN¹.

Remember that *time* is money. He that can earn² 10s. a-day by his labour, and goes abroad, or sits idle one

¹ mercante
² guadagnare (colla fatica)

half of that day, though he spends but 6d.³ during his diversion of idleness, ought not to reckon *that* the only expense; he has really spent, or rather thrown away 5s. besides.

Remember that *credit* is money. If a man lets his money lie in my hands after it is due, he gives me the interest, or so much as I can make of it during that time. This amounts to a considerable sum where a man has extensive credit, and makes good use of it.

Remember that money is of a prolific nature. Money can beget⁴ money, and its offspring⁵ can beget more, and so on⁶: — 5s. turned is 6s.: turned again it is 7s. 3d.: and so on till it becomes L. 100. The more there is of it the more it produces every turning, so that the profits rise quicker and quicker. He that kills a breeding sow⁷, destroys all her offspring to the thousandth generation. He that murders a crown, destroys all that it might have produced, even scores⁸ of pounds.

Remember that L. 6 a-year is but a groat (four pence) a day. For this little sum (which may be daily wasted either in time or expense, unperceived), a man of credit may, on his own security, have the constant possession and use of L. 100. So much in stock, briskly⁹ turned by an industrious man, produces great advantage.

Remember this saying. — " The good paymaster¹⁰ is lord of another man's purse." He that is known to pay punctually to the time he promises, may at any time, and on any occasion, raise¹¹ all the money his friends can spare¹². This is sometimes of great use. After indu-

---

³ six pence; dà l'iniziale della voce lat. *denarius denarii*
⁴ generare
⁵ prole
⁶ e così via via dicendo
⁷ troia
⁸ ventiné

⁹ prestamente, briosamente, sveltamente
¹⁰ chi paga puntualmente
¹¹ to raise (innalzare), levo (to borrow), prendere ad imprestito
¹² risparmiare

stry and frugality, nothing contributes more to the raising of a young man in the world, than punctuality and justice in all his dealings: therefore, never keep borowed money an hour beyond the time you promised, lest a disappointment shut up your friend's purse for ever.

The most trifling actions that affect a man's credit are to be regarded. The sound of your hammer[13] at five in the morning or nine at night, heard by a creditor, makes him easy six months longer; but if he sees you at a billiard table, or hears your voice at a tavern, when you should be at work, he sends for his money the next day; demands it (or a part of it) before he can receive it in a lump[14].

It shows, besides, that you are mindful[15] of what you owe: it makes you appear a careful as well as an honest man, and that still increases your credit.

Beware[16] of thinking your own that you possess, and of living accordingly. It is a mistake that many people who have credit fall into. To prevent this, keep an exact account, for some time, both of your expenses and your income. If you take the pains at first to mention particulars, it will have this good effect, you will discover how wonderfully trifling expenses mount up to large sums, and will discern what might have been, and may for the future be saved, without occasioning any great inconvenience.

In short, the way to wealth, if you desire it, is as plain as the way to market. It depends chiefly on two words, *industry* and *frugality*; that is, waste neither *time* nor *money*, but make the best use of both. Without industry and frugality nothing will do, and with them every thing[17]. He that gets[18] all he can honestly, and

---

[13] martello
[14] messe, mole, monte
[15] memore, ricordevole
[16] guardatevi
[17] will do, taciuto
[18] guadagna, ottiene.

saves all he gets (necessary expenses excepted), will certainly become *rich*.   *Franklin.*

RIVERS AND SIR HARRY.

Sir Har. Colonel, your most obedient; I am come upon the old business; for unless I am allowed to entertain hopes of Miss Rivers, I shall be the most miserable of human beings.

Riv. Sir Harry, I have already told you by letter, and I now tell you personally, I cannot listen to your proposals.

Sir Har. No, Sir?

Riv. No, Sir; I have promised my daughter to Mr. Sidney; do you know that, Sir?

Sir Har. I do; but what then? Engagements of this kind you know ——

Riv. So then, you do know that I have promised her to M. Sidney?

Sir Har. I do; but I also know that matters are not finally settled between Mr. Sidney and you; and I moreover know that his fortune is by no means equal to mine; therefore —

Riv. Sir Harry, let me ask you one question, before you make your consequence.

Sir Har. A thousand, if you please, Sir.

Riv. Why then, Sir, let me ask you, what you have ever observed in me or my conduct, that you desire me so familiarly to break my word? I thought, Sir, you considered me a man of honour.

Sir Har. And so I do, Sir, a man of the nicest [1] honour.

Riv. And yet, Sir, you ask me to violate the sanctity of my word; and tell me directly, that it is my interest to be a rascal [2].

[1] dilicato, squisito   [2] birbante

Sir Har. I really don't understand you, Colonel; I thought when I was talking to you, I was talking to a man who knew the world; and as you have not yet signed. —

Riv. Why this is mending matters with a witness! And so you think because I am not legally bound³, I am under no necessity of keeping my word? Sir Harry, laws were never made for men of honour: they want no bond but the rectitude of their own sentiments, and laws are of no use but to bind the villains of society.

Sir Har. Well! but, my dear Colonel, if you have no regard for me, show some little regard for your daughter.

Riv. I show the greatest regard for my daughter, by giving her to a man of honour; and I must not be insulted with any farther repetition of your proposals.

Sir Har. Insult you, Colonel! Is the offer of my alliance an insult? is my readiness to make what settlements⁴ you think proper. —

Riv. Sir Harry, I should consider the offer of a kingdom an insult, if it was purchased by the violation of my word: besides, though my daughter shall never go a beggar to the arms of her husband, I would rather see her happy than rich; and if she has enough to provide handsomely for a young family, and something to spare for the exigences of a worthy friend, I shall think her as affluent as if she was mistress of Mexico.

Sir. Har. Well, Colonel, I have done: but I believe —

Riv. Well, Sir Harry, and as our conference is done, we will, if you please, retire to the ladies: I shall be always glad of your acquaintance, though I cannot receive you as a son-in-law⁵; for a union of interest I look upon as a union of dishonour, and consider a marriage for money, at best, but a legal prostitution.

³ legare, obbligare; bond, legame   ⁵ (figlio in legge), genero.
⁴ stabilimenti, assegnamenti

A TRAVELLING SCENE.

A gentleman arrived at the York hotel in the city of York, one evening in the month of May, 1822 and as he had been engaged with a party of friends, he did not retire till midnight; an hour which, in that place, is not considered untimely. Having taken his place by the Highflyer Sheffield coach, which left York at half-past eight the next morning, he gave express orders to be called at half-past seven, and straightway¹ composed himself to sleep; but his rest was of short duration for, at one o'clock, he was roused² by a knocking at the door. "Who is there?" said the sleepy traveller. "Pray, sir, don't you go by the mail?" — "No I go by the Highflyer." — "Beg your pardon, sir; it's another gentleman." This unwelcome visitor robbed him of his next half hour's repose; but, after many twistings and turnings,³ he slumbered again. Scarcely had Morpheus retaken him into his service, ere a second voice saluted his ear: "Two o'clock, sir; the Express will be off in half an hour." — "What have I to do with the Express? I wish you would express yourself elsewhere." — "Lawk! sir, why I was told that you went by the Express." — "I told your master I was to go by the Highflyer, and I hope I shall hear no more of you till half-past seven." — "I ask your pardon, sir." Again he tumbled and tossed,⁴ and again he became subject to the son of Erebus: but he was doomed to be haunted. At half-past three, he heard a thundering at the door. "Sir, I have brought your boots;" you must be up in a moment, the coach is at the door." Out bounced the astonished guest, and

---

¹ addirittura
² svegliato
³ dopo molto avvoltolarsi e torcersi
⁴ avvoltolarsi e agitare.

quickly rejoined. "Why did you not speak before? I have had trouble enough with one or the other of you. Why did your master say that the coach went at half-past eight?" — "Bless me, sir, is it you who are going by the Highflyer? They told me that you went by the Nelson. Beg your pardon, sir, I am sure." In any place but York, this would have been the last customer; but the fates conspired. At five, he hears another knocking, and his patience being exhausted, he exclaims, "What the devil do you want?" A faltering female replies, "Don't you go by the Highflyer, sir?" — "To be sure I do." — "Well, sir, I'll be sure to call you at half-past seven.. Half-past seven arrived, and the gentleman made his appearance amidst a numerous assemblage of menials, all laden with petitions and apologies " Please to remember the porter, sir." — "Remember me, sir, if you please; I'm the chamber-maid, I called you, sir." — *Omnes*, " I beg pardon, sir, for disturbing you." — " Yes, I'll pardon and remember you too, when I am many miles hence." But don't you mean to give us nothing sir? — "Yes, I do mean to give you nothing; and I'll remember you all as long as I live, you may rely upon it."

ECONOMY.

A fool squanders away[1] without credit or advantage to himself more than a man of sense spends with both. The latter employs his money as he does his time: and never spends a shilling of the one or a minute of the other, but in something that is either useful or rationally pleasing to himself or others.

Without care and method, the largest fortune will not[2], and with them almost the smallest will supply all necessary expenses. As far as you can possibly, pay ready

[1] *g-lalaquere*   [2] *si sotlintende supply*

— 204 —

money³ for every thing you buy, and avoid bills⁴. Pay that money, too, yourself, and not through the hands of any servant; who always either stipulates poundage⁵ or requires a present for his good word, as they call it. Where you must have bills (as for meat and drink, clothes, etc.) pay them regularly every month, and with your own hand. Never, from a mistaken economy, buy a thing that you do not want, because it is cheap⁶; or, from a silly pride, because it is dear. Keep an account, in a book, of all that you receive, and of all that you pay; for no man who knows what he receives and what he pays ever runs out⁷. I do not mean that you should keep an account of the shillings and half crowns that you may spend in coach hire⁸, etc.; they are unworthy of the time and the ink that they would consume; leave such *minutiae* to dull penny-wisefellows: but remember, in economy, as in every other part of life, to have the proper attention to proper objects, and the proper contempt for little ones.

³ danaro contante
⁴ conto, cedola, polizza, cambiale
⁵ uno scellino per lira
⁶ a buon mercato
⁷ manca di danaro, si rovina
⁸ afflitto, uolo, pigiono
⁹ guardatevi.

EDUCATION.

I consider a human soul without education like marble in the quarry¹, which shows none of its inherent beauties, till the skill² of the polisher fetches out³ the colours, makes the surface shine, and discovers every ornamental cloud, spot and vein that run through the body of it. Education, after the same manner, when it works upon a noble mind, draws out to view every latent virtue and perfection, which without such helps are never able to make their appearance. — *Addison.*

¹ cava, patriera   ² abilità, perizia   ³ recare fuori, dare alla luce.

ON THE DUTIES OF THE YOUNG.

Let not the season of youth be barren¹ of improvements, so essential to your felicity and honour. Your character is now of your own forming; your fate is in some measure put into your own hands, Your nature is as yet pliant² and soft. Habits have not established their dominion. Prejudices have not preoccupied your understanding. The world has not had time to contract and debase your affections. All your powers are more vigorous, disembarrassed and free, than they will be at any future period. Whatever impulse you now give to your desires and passion, the direction is likely to continue. It will form the channel³ in which your life is to run; nay⁴ it may determine an everlasting issue⁵. Consider then the employment of this important period as the highest trust⁶ which shall ever be committed to you; as, in a great measure, decisive of your happiness, in time and in eternity. As in the succession of the seasons, each, by the invariable laws of nature, affects the productions of what is next in course; so, in human life, every period of our age, according as it is well or ill spent, influences the happiness of that which is to follow. Virtuous youth gradually brings forward accomplished and flourishing manhood⁷; and such manhood passes of itself, without uneasiness, into respectable and tranquil old age. But when nature is turned out of its regular course, disorder takes place in the moral, just as in the vegetable world. If the spring⁸ put forth no blossoms⁹, in summer there will be no beauty, and in

---

1 infecondo, sterile
2 per anco pieghevole
3 canale, letto di fiume
4 anzi
5 eterno esito
6 deposito
7 virilità, età virile
8 spring, primavera; summer, la state
9 blossom, fiore d'albero

autumn no fruit; so if youth be trifled away without improvement, manhood will be contemptible, and old age miserable.

Amusements, though they be of an innocent kind, require steady government, to keep them within a due and limited province. But such as are of an irregular and vicious nature, require not to be governed, but to be banished from every orderly society. As soon as a man seeks happiness from the gaming table, the midnight revel, and the other haunts[10] of licentiousness, confusion seizes upon him as its own. There will no longer be order in his family, nor order in his affairs, nor order in his time. The most important concerns of life are abandoned. Even the order of nature is by such person inverted; night is changed into day, and day into night. Character, honour, and interest itself, are trampled[11] under foot. You may with certainty prognosticate the ruin of these men to be just at hand[12]. Disorder, arisen to its height[13], has nearly accomplished its work. The spots[14] of death[15] are upon them. Let every one who would escape the pestilential contagion, fly[16] with haste[17] from their company.

Blair.

10 ridotti
11 calpest: ti.
12 alla mano, vicinissimo
13 colmo
14 macchie
15 morte
16 fuggire, volare
17 fretta.

Pleasures of literature.

Learning enables those who enjoy the benefits of it, to derive the purest, the sweetest, the most elegant, and the least injurious pleasures from themselves and from reflection. The man of taste and learning creates, as it were[1], a little world of his own, in which he exercises

1 per cosi dire

his faculties; and he feels his most exalted satisfaction arising from things the existence of which is scarcely known to the vulgar mind. Literature affords nourishment to our youth, delights our old age, adorns prosperity, supplies a refuge in adversity, is a constant source¹ of pleasure at home and abroad, and accompanies us in our travels and retirements. Amid the variety of books in our library, we may find a balsam for every wound² of the mind, and a lenient medicine for every disease.

Bacon.

¹ sorgente   ² ferita.

How to pop the question¹.

When Mr. Pickwick descended to the room² in which he and Mr. Peter Magnus had spent the preceding evening, he found that gentleman with the major part of the contents of the two bags³, the leathern hat-box⁴, and the brown paper parcel⁵ displayed to all possible advantage on his person, while he himself was pacing up and down the room in a state of the utmost excitement ad agitation.

" Good morning, Sir, " said Mr. Peter Magnus — " What do you think of this, Sir? "

" Very effective indeed, " replied Mr. Pickwick, surveying the garments of Mr. Peter Magnus with a good natured smile.

" Yes, I think it 'll do⁶, " said Mr. Magnus: ⁷ Mr. Pickwick, Sir, I have sent up my card ".

" Have you? " said Mr. Pickwick.

¹ How to ask a lady's hand
² stanza
³ sacchetti
⁴ cappelliera
⁵ pacchetto, plico, fagotto
⁶ farò (il mio affare)
⁷ sottinteso, sent

"Yes; and the waiter brought back word*, that she would see me at eleven — at eleven, Sir; it only wants a quarter now ".

"Very near the time," said Mr. Pickwick.

"Yes, it is rather near," replied Mr. Magnus, "rather too near to be pleasant, — eh! Mr. Pickwick, Sir?"

"Confidence is a great thing in these cases," observed Mr. Pickwick.

"I believe it is, Sir," said Mr. Peter Magnus. "I am very confident, Sir. Really, Mr. Pickwick, I do not see why a man should feel any fear in such a case as this, sir. What is it, sir? There's nothing to be ashamed of; it's a matter of mutual accommodation, nothing more. Husband on one side, wife on the other. That's my view of the matter, Mr. Pickwick ".

"It is a very philosophical one," replied Mr. Pickwick. "But breakfast is waiting*, Mr. Magnus. Come ".

Down they sat to breakfast; but it was evident, notwithstanding the boasting of Mr. Peter Magnus, that he laboured under a very considerable degree of nervousness, of which loss of appetite, a propensity to upset[10] the tea-things, a spectral attempt at drollery[11], and an irresistible inclination to look at the clock every other[12] second, were among the principal symptoms.

"He — he — he," tittered[13] Mr. Magnus, affecting cheerfulness, and gasping[14] with agitation. "It only wants two minutes, Mr. Pickwick. Am I pale, Sir?"

"Not very" replied Mr. Pickwik.

There was a brief pause.

"I beg your pardon, Mr. Pickwick; but have you ever done this sort of thing in your time? " said Mr. Magnus.

---

* parola, risposta
* aspettare, attendere
[10] rovesciare
[11] facezia, allegria
[12] ogni (altro) due
[13] sorridere, ridere con poco rumore
[14] boccheggiare

"You mean proposing?" said Mr. Pickwick.

"Yes".

"Never," said Mr. Pickwick, with great energy, "never".

"You have no idea, then, how it's best to begin?" said Mr. Magnus.

"Why", said Mr. Pickwick, "I may have formed some ideas upon the subject, but, as I have never submitted them to the test of experience, I should be sorry if you were induced to regulate your proceedings by them".

"I should feel very much obliged to you, for any advice, Sir," said Mr. Magnus, taking another look at the clock, the hand[13] of which was verging on[14] the five minutes past.

"Well, Sir," said Mr. Pickwick, with the profound solemnity with which that great man could when he pleased, render his remarks so deeply impressive — "I should commence, Sir, with a tribute,to the lady's beauty and excellent qualities; from them, Sir, I should diverge to my own unworthiness".

"Very good," said Mr. Magnus.

"Unworthiness for *her* only, mind", Sir," resumed Mr. Pickwick; "for to shew that I was not wholly unworthy, Sir, I should take a brief review[15] of my past life, and present condition. I should argue, by analogy, that to anybody else I must be a very desirable object. I should then expatiate[17] on the warmth of my love, and the depth of my devotion. Perhaps I might then be tempted to seize[20] her hand".

"Yes, I see," said Mr. Magnus; "that would be a very great point".

"I should then, Sir, continued Mr. Pickwick, growing warmer as the subject presented itself in more

---

[13] Indice, lancetta dell'orologio
[15] tirava verso
[17] badate bene
[14] rivista, esame
[19] discorrere distesamente
[20] afferrare

glowing²¹ colours before him — " I should then, Sir, come " to the plain and simple question," Will you have me? I think I am justified in assuming that, upon this, she would turn away her head ".

" You think that may be taken for granted "? " said Mr. Magnus; " because, if she did not do that at the right place, it would be embarrassing ".

" I think she would " said Mr. Pickwick. " Upon this, Sir, I should squeeze²³ her hand; and I think — I *think*, Mr. Magnus — that after I had done that, supposing there was no refusal, I should gently draw away the handkerchief²⁴, which my slight knowledge of human nature leads me to suppose the lady would be applying to her eyes at the moment, and steal a respectful kiss²⁵. I think I should kiss her, Mr. Magnus; and at this particular point, I am decidedly of opinion that if the lady were going to take me at all, she would murmur into my ears a bashful²⁶ acceptance ".

Mr. Magnus started²⁷, gazed on Mr. Pickwick's intelligent face, for a short time in silence, and then (the dial pointing to the ten minutes past) shook²⁸ him warmly by the hand, and rushed desperately²⁹ from the room.

Mr. Pickwick had taken a few strides to and fro³⁰, and the small hand of the clock following the latter part of his example, had arrived at the figure which indicates the half hour, when the door suddenly opened. He turned round to greet³¹ Mr. Peter Magnus, and encountered in his stead the joyous face of Mr. Tupman, the serene countenance of Mr. Winkle, and the intellectual lineaments of Mr. Snodgrass.

²¹ caldi, ardenti, risplendenti
²² concesso, certo, evidente
²³ stringerei
²⁴ tirerei via il fazzoletto
²⁵ bacio
²⁶ timida, schiva, modesta
²⁷ balzò in piedi
²⁸ scosse, strinse
²⁹ uscì di slancio, da disperato
³⁰ passi lunghi andando e ritornando (a traverso la camera)
³¹ salutare

As Mr. Pickwick greeted them, Mr. Peter Magnus tripped into³¹ the room.
" My friends. the gentleman I was speaking of, Mr. Magnus," said Mr. Pickwick.
" Your most obedient, gentlemen, said Mr. Magnus, evidently in a high state of excitement; Mr. Pickwick, allow me to speak to you, one moment, Sir ".
As he said this, Mr. Magnus harnessed his fore-finger to Mr. Pickwick's buttonhole³³, and, drawing him into a window recess, said —
" Congratulate me, Mr. Pickwick; I followed your advice to the very letter ".
" And it was all correct, was it ? " inquired Mr. Pickwick.
" It was, Sir — could not possibly have been better, replied Mr. Magnus; Mr. Pickwick, she is mine ".
" I congratulate you, with all my heart," replied Mr. Pickwick, warmly shaking his new friend by the hand.
" You must see her, Sir, " said Mr. Magnus; " this way³⁴, if you please. Excuse us for one instant, gentlemen ". And hurrying on in this way. Mr. Peter Magnus drew Mr. Pickwick from the room. He paused at the next door in the passage, and tapped ³⁵ gently thereat.
" Come in," said a female voice. And in they went.
" Miss Witherfield," said Mr. Magnus, ' allow me to introduce my very particular friend, Mr. Pickwick, I beg to make you known to Miss Witherfield ".

Dickens.

³² entrò saltellando
³³ ficcò il dito indice nella bottoniera del signor P.
³⁴ da qui
³⁵ picchiò.

A PALACE IN ABYSSINIA.

The place which the wisdom or policy of antiquity had destined for the residence of the Abyssinian princes was a spacious valley in the kingdom of Amhara, surrounded on every side by mountains, of which the summits overhang the middle part. The only passage by which it could be entered was a cavern that passed under a rock, of which it had been long disputed whether it was the work of nature or of human industry. The outlet¹ of the cavern was concealed by a thick wood, and the mouth which opened into the valley was closed by gates of iron, forged² by the artificers of ancient days, so massy, that no man, without the help of engines, could open or shut them. From the mountains, on every side, rivulets descended, that filled all the valley with verdure and fertility, and formed a lake in the middle, inhabited by fish of every species, and frequented by every fowl which nature has taught to dip the wing in water. This lake discharged its superfluities by a stream which entered a dark cleft⁴ of the mountain on the northern side, and fell, with dreadful noise, from precipice to precipice, till it was heard no more. The sides of the mountains were covered with trees; the banks of the brooks⁵ were diversified with flowers; every blast shook spices from the rocks;⁶ and every month dropped fruits upon the ground.

All animals that bite the grass or browse the shrub,⁷ whether wild or tame, wandered in this extensive circuit, secured from the beasts of prey by the mountains which confined them. On one part were flocks and herds feeding in the pastures; on another, all the beasts of chase frisking in the lawns;⁸ the sprightly kid⁹ was bounding on the rocks; the subtle monkey frolicking in the trees; and the solemn elephant reposing in the shade. All the diversities of the world were brought together; the blessings of nature were collected, and its evils extracted

¹ uscita
² lavorato
³ macchina
⁴ fessura
⁵ ruscello

⁶ ogni sbuffo di vento manda aromi dalle rocce
⁷ pascola tra gli arbusti
⁸ da caccia saltellanti nei pratelli
⁹ capretto

and excluded. The valley, wide and fruitful, supplied its inhabitants with the necessaries of life, and all delights and superfluities were added at the annual visit which the emperor paid his children, when the iron gate was opened to the sound of music; and during eight days every one that resided in the valley was required to propose whatever might contribute to make seclusion pleasant, to fill up the vacancies of attention, and lessen the tediousness of time. Every desire was immediately granted. All the artificers of pleasure were called to gladden[10] the festivity: the musicians exerted the power of harmony, and the dancer showed their activity before the princes, in hopes that they should pass their lives in this blissful captivity, to which those only were admitted whose performance was thought able to add novelty to luxury. Such was the appearance of security and delight which this retirement afforded, that those to whom it was new, always desired that it might be perpetual; and as those on whom the iron gate had once closed, were never suffered to return, the effect of longer experience could not be known. Thus every year produced new schemes of delight, and new competitors for imprisonment.

The palace stood on an eminence raised about thirty paces above the surface of the lake. It was divided into many squares,[11] or courts, built with greater or less magnificence, according to the rank of those for whom they were designed. The roofs[12] were turned into arches of massy stone, joined by a cement that grew harder by time; and the building stood from century to century, deriding the solstitial rains and equinoctial hurricanes,[13] without need of reparation. This house, which was so large as to be fully known to none but some ancient

[10] rallegrare
[11] piazze
[12] tetti
[13] temporali.

officers, who successively inherited the secrets of the place, was built as if suspicion herself had dictated the plan. To every room there was an open and a secret passage; every square had a communication with the rest, either from the upper stories by private galleries, or by subterranean passages from the lower apartments. Many of the colums had unsuspected cavities, in which a long race of monarchs had deposited their treasures. They then closed up the opening with marble, which was never to be removed but in the utmost exigencies of the kingdom; and recorded their accumulations in a book, which was itself concealed in a tower, not entered but by the emperor, attended by the prince who stood next in succession.

(Johnson.)

THE STORMING[1] OF FRONT-DE-BŒUF'S CASTLE.

Following with wonderful promptitude the directions of Ivanhoe, and availing herself of the protection of the large ancient shield,[2] which she placed against the lower part of the window, Rebecca with tolerable security to herself could witness part of what was passing without the castle, and report to Ivanhoe the preparations which the assailed were making for the storm.

"The skirts[3] of the wood seem lined with archers although only a few are advanced from its dark shadow."

"Under what banner[4]?" asked Ivanhoe.

"Under no ensign of war which I can observe," answered Rebecca.

"A singular novelty," muttered the knight, "to advance to storm such a castle without pennon or banner displayed! Seest thou who they be that act as leaders[5]?"

[1] assalto
[2] scudo
[3] estremità
[4] bandiera
[5] conduttore

"A knight clad in sable armour⁶ is the most conspicuous," said the Jewess; "he alone is armed from head to heel, and seems to assume the direction of all around him."

"What device⁷ does he bear on his shield?" replied Ivanhoe.

"Something resembling a bar⁸ of iron, and a padlock⁹ painted blue on the block shield."

"A fetterlock and shacklebolt¹⁰ azure," said Ivanhoe; "I know not who may bear the device, but well I ween" it might now be mine own. Canst thou not see the motto?"

"Scarce the device itself at this distance," replied Rebecca, "but when the sun glances fair upon his shield it shows as I tell you."

"Seem there no other leaders?" exclaimed the anxious inquirer.

"None of mark and distinction that I can behold from this station," said Rebecca, "but doubtless the other side of the castle is also assailed. They appear even now preparing to advance."

Her description was here suddenly interrupted by the signal for assault, which was given by the blast of a shrill bugle,¹² and at once answered by a flourish¹³ of the Norman trumpets from the battlements.

"And I must lie here," exclaimed Ivanhoe, "while the game that gives me freedom or death, is played out by the hand of others! — Look from the window once again, kind maiden, but beware that you are not marked by the archers beneath. — Look out once more, and

⁶ un cavaliere vestito di bruna armatura
⁷ divisa
⁸ sbarra
⁹ lucchetto
¹⁰ sbarra di ferro e catenaccio
¹¹ m'immagino
¹² dal soffiar di uno strillante corno
¹³ suono

tell me if they yet advance to the storm. What dost thou see, Rebecca?"

"Nothing but the cloud of arrows, flying so thick as to dazzle mine eyes, and to hide the bowmen¹² who shoot them."

"That cannot endure," said Ivanhoe; "if they press not right on, to carry the castle by force of arms, the archery may avail but little against stone walls and bulwarks. Look for the Knight of Fetterlock, fair Rebecca, and see how he bears himself; for, as the leader is, so will his followers be."

"I see him not," said Rebecca.

"Foul craven!¹³" exclaimed Ivanhoe, "does he blench from the helm¹⁴, when the wind blows highest?"

"He blenches not! he blenches not!" said Rebecca. "I see him now: he leads a body of men under the outer barrier of the barbican. They pull down the palisades: they hew down the barriers with axes. His high black plume floats abroad over the throng¹⁷, like a raven¹⁸ over the field of the slain. They have made a breach in the barriers—they rush in—they are thrust back! Front-de-Bœuf heads the defenders; I see his gigantic form above the press. They throng again to the breach, and the pass is disputed hand to hand, and man to man. God of Jacob! it is the meeting of two fierce tides—the conflict of two oceans moved by adverse winds."

She turned her head from the lattice,¹⁹ as if unable longer to endure a sight so terrible.

"Look forth again, Rebecca," said Ivanhoe, mistaking the cause of her retiring; "the archery must in some degree have ceased, since they are now fighting hand to hand—there is now less danger."

¹² arcieri
¹³ indegno poltrone
¹⁴ indietreggia dal timore
¹⁷ calca
¹⁸ corvo
¹⁹ ingraticciata

Rebecca again looked forth, and almost immediately exclaimed, "Holy Prophets of the law! Front-de-Bœuf and the Black Knight fight hand to hand on the breach, amid the roar of their followers, who watch the progress of their strife. Heaven strike with the cause of the oppressed and the captive!"—She then uttered a loud shriek and exclaimed, "He is down! he is down!"

"Who is down?" cried Ivanhoe, "for our dear Lady's sake, tell me which has fallen?"

"The Black Knight," answered Rebecca, faintly, then instantly again shouted with joyful eagerness—"But no —but no!—the name of the Lord of Hosts be blessed! he is on foot again, and fights as if there were twenty men's strength in his single arm. His sword is broken —he snatches an axe from a yeoman—he presses Front-de-Bœuf with blow on blow. — The giant stoops, and totters like an oak under the steel of the woodman—he falls, —he falls!"

"Front-de-Bœuf?" exclaimed Ivanhoe.

"Front-de-Bœuf!" answered the Jewess; "his men rush to the rescue, headed by the haughty Templar; their united force compels the champion to pause. They drag[10] Front-de-Bœuf within the walls."

"The assailants have won the barriers, have they not?" said Ivanhoe.

"They have—they have—and they press the besieged hard upon the outer wall; some plant ladders,[11] some swarm[12] like bees, and endeavour to ascend upon the shoulders of each other—down go stones, beams, and trunks of trees upon their heads; and, as fast as they bear the wounded to the rear,[13] fresh men supply their place in the assault—Great God! hast thou given men thine own image, that it should be thus cruelly defaced by the hands of their brethren!"

[10] trascinano [11] collocano scale [12] brulicano [13] indietro

"Think not of that," replied Ivanhoe, "this is no place for such thoughts.—Who yield?—who push their way¹⁴?"

"The ladders are thrown down," replied Rebecca, shuddering, "the soldiers lie groveling²⁵ under them like crushed reptiles—the besieged have the better."

"Saint George strike for us!" said the Knight, "do the false yeomen give way?"

"No!" exclaimed Rebecca, "they bear themselves right yeomanly—the Black Knight approaches the postern²⁶ with his huge axe—the thundering blows which he deals you may hear them above all the din and shouts²⁷ of the battle—Stones and beams are hailed down on the bold champion—he regards them no more than if they were thistledown,²⁸ or feathers."

"By Saint John of Acre!" said Ivanhoe, raising himself joyfully in his couch,²⁹ "methought there was but one man in England that might do such a deed."

"The postern gate shakes," continued Rebecca; "it crashes — it is splintered by his blows³⁰—they rush in —the out-work is won—O God, they hurl the defenders from the battlements—they throw them into the moat— O men! if ye be men, indeed, spare them that can resist no longer."

"The bridge—the bridge which communicates with the castle,—have they won that pass?" exclaimed Ivanhoe.

"No," replied Rebecca, "the Templar has destroyed the plank on which they crossed— few of the defenders escaped with him into the castle—the shrieks and cries, which you hear, tell the fate of the others."

(*Valter Scott.*)

²⁴ chi cede, chi avanza ?   ²⁸ cardoni
²⁵ striscianto   ²⁹ letto
²⁶ posteria   ³⁰ è schiantato e ridotto in pezzi dai
²⁷ schiamazzo e frastuono   suoi colpi.

VOCABOLARIO

DELLE PAROLE PIÙ DIFFICILI E MENO RIPETUTE NEL METODO [*]

INGLESE - ITALIANO.

A

Abide (to), *dimorare*.
Abruptly, *improvvisamente*.
Advertisement, *annunzio*.
Advisable, *prudente*.
Afford (to), *fornire*.
Alehouse, *birraria*.
Answer, *risposta*.
Apologize (to), *chieder scusa*.
Astonishment, *stupore*.
Atone for (to), *espiare*.
Avert (to), *stornare*.

B

Bag, *sacco*.
Balance (to), *saldare il conto corrente*.
Base, *vile*.
Beaver, *castore*.
Beam, *raggio*.
Bee, *ape*.
Beget (to), *generare acquistare*.
Beforehand, *anticipatamente*.
Behave (to), *comportarsi*.
Bequeath (to), *lasciar in eredità*.
Betray (to), *tradire, dimostrare*.
Betimes, *per tempo*.
Bewail (to), *compiangere*.
Bill of lading, *polizza di carico*.
Blast (to), *distrugger la riputazione*.
Blemish, *macchia, difetto*.
Bleed (to), *levar sangue*.
Blockhead, *imbecille*.
Blush (to), *arrossire*.
Board on (to), *stare a pensione*.
Borrow (to), *prender imprestito*
Both, *ambidue, tanto per.... che*.
Bower, *pergolato*.
Breath (to), *respirare*.
Bribe (to), *corrompere*.
Broker, *rigattiere*.
Brook, *ruscello*.
Bush, *cespuglio*.
Bustle, *trambusto, briga*.

C

Cage, *gabbia*.
Cap, *berretta*.

[*] I verbi irregolari essendo già disposti in tabella nel corso del metodo, non fanno parte di questo vocabolario.

Cash, *denaro contante.*
Challenge, *sfida.*
Charge (to), *far pagare.*
Chatt (to), *ciarlare.*
Chattels, *beni mobili.*
Cheek, *guancia.*
Cheese, *formaggio.*
Chessboard, *scacchiera.*
Christmass, *natale.*
Clearsighted, *di buona vista.*
Close, *fitto, spesso, rasente.*
Closet, *gabinetto.*
Coal, *carbone.*
Cobbler, *ciabattino.*
Comb (to), *pettinare.*
Conceal (to), *nascondere.*
Corn, *grano.*
Covet (to), *desiderare con ardore.*
Crowd, *folla.*
Cursed, *maledetto.*

D

Dear me, *povero me.*
Deceased, *defunto.*
Deserve (to), *meritare.*
Detect (to), *scoprire.*
Dirty, *sudicio, insudiciare*
Disguise, *travestimento.*
Donkey, *somaro.*
Drawing-room, *salotto.*
Dressing-gown, *veste da camera.*
Dupe, *zimbello.*
Dust, *polvere.*
Dutch, *olandese.*

E

Eagerly, *con ardore.*
Ear, *orecchio.*
Earn (to), *guadagnare col lavoro.*

Eating-house, *locanda.*
Eddy, *vortice.*
Elsewhere, *altrove.*
Embroidery, *ricamo.*
Enclose (to), *includere.*
Endeavour (to), *tentare.*
Enough, *abbastanza.*
Enliven (to), *dar vita.*
Exchange, *borsa (d'affari).*
Explain (to), *spiegare.*
Exertion, *fatica.*

F

Fair, *bello.*
Fancy (to), *immaginarsi.*
Far, *lontano.*
Fate, *destino.*
Fear (to), *temere.*
Fee, *spese.*
Fit (to), *adattare.*
Forward (to), *promuovere.*
Friar, *frate.*
Fright, *timore, spaventare.*
Frost, *gelo.*

G

Game, *partita, selvaggina.*
Gate, *cancello.*
Gift, *dono.*
Glad, *contento.*
Grape, *uva.*
Greedy, *ingordo.*
Groan (to), *gemere.*
Gruffily, *rozzamente.*
Gun, *schioppo, cannone.*

H

Hair, *capelli.*
Hay, *fieno.*

— 221 —

Ham, *prosciutto.*
Haste, *fretta.*
He-goat, *caprone.*
Hence, *da qui.*
Highroad, *strada maestra.*
Hire (to), *noleggiare.*
Holyday, *festa.*
Hurrican, *temporale.*
Hurry, *fretta.*
Hurt (to), *farsi male.*

I

Ill treat (to), *maltrattare.*
Improvement, *miglioramento.*
Inn, *albergo.*
Inkstand, *calamaio.*
Inquire (to), *ricercare.*
Instead, *invece.*
Island, *isola.*
Invoice, *fattura.*

J

Join (to), *raggiungere.*
Joiner, *falegname.*
Just, *appunto, giusto.*

K

Key, *chiave.*
Kingdom, *regno.*
Kitchen, *cucina.*
Knock (to), *battere.*

L

Lad, *giovinetto.*
Ladder, *scala a piuoli.*
Land (to), *approdare.*
Last, *ultimo, durare.*
Late, *defunto.*

Laziness, *pigrizia.*
Leave, *congedo, permesso.*
Lecture, *lettura, rimprovero.*
Lest, *per timore che.*
Lie (to), *mentire, menzogna.*
Light - headed, *sventato.*
Likely, *probabilmente.*
Little-sized, *di piccola statura.*
Loan, *prestito.*
Lock, *riccio.*
Lodging, *alloggio.*
Loft, *soffitta.*
Low, *basso.*
Lull (to), *quetare, addormentare.*

M

Mad *passo arrabbiato.*
Male, *maschio.*
Meal, *pasto.*
Mean, *mezzo, significare.*
Meaning, *senso.*
Meanwhile (in the), *frattanto*
Methink, *mi pare.*
Methought, *mi pareva.*
Mild, *mite.*
Milliner, *modista.*
Miror, *specchio.*
Mistake, *errore, ingannarsi.*
Monkey, *scimmia.*
Morning, *mattina.*
Mourning, *lutto.*
Murder, *omicidio.*
Mushrooms, *funghi.*

N

Nail, *chiodo.*
Naked, *nudo.*
Napkin, *tovagliuolo.*
Nay, *anzi.*

Nearly, *quasi, circa.*
Neck, *collo.*
Newspaper, *giornale.*
Noise, *rumore.*
Notwithstanding, *nondimeno.*
Nowhere, *in nessun luogo.*
Nuts, *noci.*

O

Odd, *strano, ridicolo.*
Of course, *certamente naturalmente.*
Once, *una volta.*
Otherwise, *altrimenti.*
Overtake (to), *raggiungere,*

P

Padlock, *lucchetto.*
Parcel, *pacchetto.*
Partridge, *pernice.*
Pattern, *campione.*
Perceive (to), *scorgere.*
Perform (to), *adempire.*
Plate, *tondo.*
Pride, *orgoglio.*
Provided, *purché,*
Purchase, *comprata.*
Purpose, *scopo, proposito.*
Pursue (to), *perseguitare.*
Puzzle (to), *imbrogliare.*

Q

Quail, *quaglia.*
Quarry, *cava petriera.*
Quench (to), *estinguere la sete.*

R

Railway, *ferrovia.*
Ransom, *riscatto.*

Rascal, *birbone.*
Raven, *corvo.*
Rash, *impetuoso.*
Receipt, *ricevuta.*
Recipe, *ricetta.*
Recovery, *guarigione.*
Relapse (to), *ricadere.*
Release (to), *liberare.*
Remove (to), *sloggiare.*
Requite (to), *ricompensare.*
Roguery, *furfanteria.*
Roof, *tetto.*
Rouse (to), *destare.*

S

Sad, *triste.*
Saucer, *piattino.*
Saucepan, *cassuola.*
Scarcely, *appena.*
Security, *garanzia:*
Selfish, *egoista.*
Shamefully, *vergognosamente.*
Shape, *forma.*
Sheet, *foglio.*
Shelter (to), *ripararsi.*
Shield, *scudo.*
Shoulder, *spalla.*
Shortsighted, *miope.*
Silk, *seta.*
Snuff-box, *tabacchiera.*
Song, *canzone.*
Soul, *anima.*
Spoon, *cucchiaio.*
Sport, *divertimento.*
Squander away, *scialacquare.*
Square, *piazza.*
Staff, *bastone, stato maggiore.*
Staircase, *scala.*
Star, *stella.*

Starve (to), *morir di fame.*
Steam, *vapore.*
Stock, *capitale.*
Stout, *forte, robusto.*
Story, *piano (di casa).*
Straight on, *diretto, avanti.*
Suit (to), *convenire.*
Summer, *estate.*

T

Table-cloth, *tovaglia.*
Talk (to), *parlare.*
Tedious, *noioso.*
Thankfulness, *gratitudine.*
Thoroughly, *completamente.*
Thunder-bolt, *fulmine.*
Tired, *stanco.*
Tongs, *molle.*
Trust, *fiducia.*
Towards, *verso.*
Turn (to), *volgersi, rivolgersi.*

U

Under, *sotto.*
Umpire, *arbitro.*
Uneasy (to be), *essere inquieto.*
Unless, *a meno che.*
Upper, *superiore.*
Upset (to), *rovesciare.*
Utter (to), *pronunciare.*

V

Valley, *valle.*
Vegetables, *legumi.*
Victuals, *vivande.*
View (to), *esaminare.*

W

Wafer, *ostia.*
Wag, *burlone.*
Wager, *scommessa.*
Waiscoat, *giubbetto.*
Wait upòn (to) *andar a trovare.*
Wall, *muro.*
Water (to), *inaffiare.*
Weather, *tempo (di atmosfera).*
Wet, *umido.*
Whilst, *mentre.*
Whip (to), *sferzare.*
Wholsale, *all' ingrosso.*
Wicked, *malvagio.*
Will, *testamento.*
Wing, *ala.*
Witness, *testimonio.*
Wonder (to), *maravigliarsi.*
Wood, *legno, bosco.*
Worship (to), *adorare.*
Wretched, *miserabile.*

ITALIANO - INGLESE.

A

Abbastanza, *enough.*
Adagio, *slowly.*
Adorare, *to worship.*
Adunanza, *meeting.*

Acchetare, *to still.*
Accludere, *to enclose.*
Ala, *wing.*
Alto, *high, tall.*
Altrove, *elsewhere.*
Ambidue, *both.*

— 224 —

Annunzio, *advertisement.*
Angolo, *corner.*
Anzi, *nay.*
Anticipatamente, *in advance, beforehand.*
Arbitro, *umpire.*
Arrampicarsi, *to creep.*
Arrossire, *to blush.*
Asciutto, *dry.*

B

Barcaiuolo, *waterman.*
Basso, *low base.*
Bianco, *white.*
Birraria, *alehouse, public house.*
Borsa (d'affari), *exchange.*
Bosco, *wood.*

C

Calamaio, *inkstand.*
Calcagno, *heel.*
Cameriera, *house-maid.*
Cancello, *gate.*
Casseruola, *saucepan.*
Castoro, *beaver.*
Cavarsela, *to come off.*
Chiacchierare, *to gossip, to chatt.*
Ciabattino, *cobbler.*
Colpire, *to hit.*
Comodino, *night-table.*
Comportarsi, *to behave.*
Collo, *neck.*
Condotta, *behaviour.*
Congedo, *leave.*
Convenire, *to suit.*
Coperta, *quilt.*
Cuore, *heart.*

D

Dado, *die.*
Defunto, *late deceased.*
Dibattimento, *trial.*
Dietro, *behind.*
Dimora, *abode stay.*
Domani, *to-morrow.*
Dono, *gift, present.*
Durare, *to last.*

E

Egoista, *selfish.*
Epoca, *age.*
Erba, *grass.*
Errore, *mistake.*
Espiare, *to atone for.*
Estinguere, *to quench.*

F

Fagiano, *pheasant.*
Falegname, *joiner.*
Fattura, *invoice.*
Fazzoletto, *handkerchief.*
Femmina, *female.*
Festa, *holyday.*
Fieno, *hay.*
Finalment, *at last.*
Finchè, *until.*
Foglio, *sheet.*
Folla, *crowd.*
Forchetta, *fork.*
Formaggio, *cheese.*
Fornire, *to afford.*
Fragola, *strawberry.*
Frattanto, *in the meanwhile.*
Freccia, *arrow.*
Fulmine, *thunder-bolt.*

G

Gabbia, *cage.*
Gabinetto, *closet.*
Garanzia, *security.*
Gelo, *frost.*
Gemere, *to groan.*
Giubbetto, *waistcoat.*
Gradire, *to like.*
Gratitudine, *thankfulness.*
Guastare, *to spoil,*
Gusto, *taste.*

I

Impetuoso, *rash.*
Inaffiare, *to water.*
Inedia, *want.*
Incirca, *about, nearly.*
Ingannare, *to cheat, to deceive.*
Ingannarsi, *to mistake, to be mistaken.*
Ingrosso (all'), *wholsale.*
Introdurre, *to introduce, to show into.*
Invece, *instead.*

L

Lagrima, *tear.*
Lamentare, *to complain.*
Lavoro, *work.*
Lettiera, *bedstead.*
Lutto, *mourning.*

M

Maestro, *master, teacher.*
Maledetto, *cursed.*
Mare, *sea.*
Meravigliarsi, *to wonder.*

Meritare, *to deserve.*
Mattina, *morning.*
Mazzetto, *nosegay.*
Mercanzia, *marchandise, ware.*
Mezzodi, *noon.*
Mobilia, *furniture.*
Molle (da fuoco), *tongs.*
Mutande, *trawsers.*

N

Nascere, *to be born.*
Nascondere, *to conceal.*
Noioso, *tiresome.*
Noleggiare, *to hire.*

O

Oca, *goose.*
Occhiali, *spectacles.*
Omicidio, *murder.*
Orecchio, *ear.*
Ostia, *wafer.*

P

Paglia, *straw.*
Palco (del teatro), *box.*
Partita, *game.*
Pasqua, *easter.*
Permesso, *leave, permission.*
Pesce, *fish.*
Pettinare, *to comb.*
Platea, *pit.*
Podere, *farm.*
Polizza di carico, *bill of lading.*
Prender imprestito, *to borrow.*
Primavera, *spring.*
Privare, *bereave.*
Pulito, *neat,*
Purchè, *provided.*
Pure, *even, also.*

Q

Quaglia, *quail.*
Quasi, *almost, nearly.*

R

Raccogliere, *to gather, to pick up.*
Raffreddore, *cold.*
Raggio, *beam.*
Respirare, *to breath.*
Restituire, *to give back.*
Ricetta, *recipe.*
Riconoscere, *to acknowledge.*
Rifugiarsi, *to take refuge.*
Riscatto, *ransom.*
Rivolgere, *to turn.*
Rovesciare, *to overst.*
Rumore, *noise.*

S

Sacco, *bag.*
Salire (le scale), *to go up stairs.*
Salvietta, *napkin.*
Sanguinario, *blood-minded.*
Scacchi, *chess.*
Scacchiera, *chess-board.*
Scala, *staircase.*
Scendere (le scale', *to go down stairs.*
Selvaggina, *game.*
Seppellire, *to burry.*
Seta, *silk.*
Sinistro, *left.*
Sottana, *gown.*
Sotto, *under.*
Spalla, *shoulder.*
Stagione, *season.*
Stella, *star.*

Stolto, *fool,*
Stornare, *to avert.*
Strano, *odd.*
Strillare, *to scream.*
Stupore, *astonishment.*
Superiore, *upper.*
Supplicare, *to beseech.*

T

Tabacchiera, *snuff box.*
Tela, *linen.*
Tentare, *to try.*
Testa, *head.*
Testamento, *will.*
Tondo, *plate.*
Torto, *wrong.*
Trafficare, *to deal.*
Tramandare, *to hand down.*
Trambusto, *bustle.*
Triste, *sad.*
Tuttavia, *however, notwithstanding yet.*

U

Uccello, *bird.*
Ultimo, *last.*
Umido, *wet.*
Usignuolo, *nightingale.*

V

Valoroso, *gallant.*
Valorosamente, *bravely.*
Vergognarsi, *to be ashamed.*
Veste da camera, *dressing-gown.*
Vento, *wind.*
Vile, *base coward.*
Vertice, *eddy.*

INDICE RAGIONATO

DELLE MATERIE CONTENUTE NEL METODO. [*]

Dell'articolo determinativo

	Pagina	Esercizio
Declinazione dell'articolo.	15 e seg.	1 e seg.
Si sopprime avanti a) agli aggettivi e pronomi possessivi	25 »	13 »
» » b) ai nomi propri e geografici.	113, 10	91, 265
» » c) ai sostantivi presi in senso generale	9	»
Si aggiunge innanzi ai numeri ordinali	428	101
Si cambia in aggettivo possessivo innanzi ai sostantivi esprimenti parti del corpo ed oggetti di vestiario.	150	121

Articolo indeterminativo

A avanti consonante an avanti a vocale.	17	5
Serve per distributivo.	157	126
Differenza tra l'art. ind. e il numerale one.	8	263
Si aggiunge ai nomi di professione e patria	»	»
A (o) one si aggiungono avanti a hundred, e thousand quando non son preceduti da altri numeri	146	94
Sua speciale posizione dopo alcune parole.	12	267

Sostantivo

Formazione del plurale coll'aggiunta della lettera s.	10	0
Formazione del plurale coll'aggiunta della sillaba es.	46	33

[*] Per dare una maggior sintesi all'esposizione delle regole nell' Indice ho indicato cumulativamente le regole esposte nel primo e secondo volume; dal numero dell'esercizio si conosce se la citazione si riferisce al 1° o al 2° volume.

	Pagina	Esercizio
Diverse eccezioni si trovano nei seguenti esercizi.	—	14, 15, 25 37, 39, 71 153 e 155
Genere dei sostantivi	59	47
Formazione di alcuni femminini.	310	231
Del partitivo	138	408
Genitivo possessivo.	57, 308	45, 231
Nomi dei giorni della settimana.	128, 429	104, 103
Nomi dei mesi	429	103
Sostantivi cambiati in aggettivi mediante l'aggiunta di alcune terminazioni.	19, 451	273, 368
Sostantivi concreti si cambiano in astratti mediante l'aggiunta di alcune terminazioni. .	451	366
Il sostantivo può essere rappresentato dalle parole *one ones* dopo l'aggettivo.	323	248

Dell'aggettivo qualificativo

È invariabile	15	—1
Si mette prima del sostantivo.	16	3
Eccezioni a questa regola	28	281
Formazione del superlativo assoluto con la parola *very*	31	23
Gradi di comparazione	86 e seg.	65 e seg.
Comparativi e superlativi irregolari	172	136
Non può far le veci del sostantivo eccetto che nel plurale in senso generale.	172	136
Aggettivi e pronomi possessivi	25, 27, 105	13, 17, 80
Aggettivi o pronomi dimostrativi	31	23
Si sopprimono avanti a un genitivo possessivo.	80	65
Si traducono col pronome personale quando si riferiscono a persone ed è seguito dal relativo.	167	103

Pronome personale

Genere e caso.	59, 81	47, 63
Posto dell'accusativo	59	47
L'accusativo si antepone al dativo	123	99
Posto eccezionale del soggetto	17	274
Costui colui ecc	18	297
Pronome impersonale *si*.	262	201
Pronomi reciproci	274	209
» riflessivi e asseverativi.	279	213

— 220 —

	Pagina	Esercizio
Il pronome dimostrativo e aggettivo possessivo non stanno assieme	31	289
Pronome relativo	36	25
Si deve tradurre con *that*	38	239
Declinazione del relativo *who*	60	49
Numeri ordinali. Loro formazione ed uso; vanno preceduti dall'articolo determinativo	128	101

Verbo

Ausiliare. Tabella degli ausiliari avere ed essere, forma affermativa, negativa interrogativa e interrogativa-negativa	217	—
Tabella della congiunzione del verbo regolare forma affermativa, negativa, interrogativa e interrogativa-negativa	253	—
Formazione del presente indicativo forma afferm.	69	54
» » » » interrogativa e negativa	97	74
Passato; una sola forma pel perf. ed imperf.	37	27
Formazione del participio passato o passato indicativo del verbi regolari	113	87
Interrogativo e negativo anche per gli irreg.	168	129
Formazione del futuro	184	143
» del condizionale	220	171
» dell'imperativo	236	188
» del presente soggiuntivo	238	192
» del passato »	272, 238	173, 192
Verbi irregolari (tabella)	243	—
Verbi riflessivi	270	213
Tabella de' verbi riflessivi in italiano e non riflessivi in inglese	92	333
Verbi reciproci	94	335

Difettivi.

May e can	268	195
Must	269	203
Ought	272	207
Un verbo si cambia in sostantivo coll'aggiunta della sillaba *er*	57	303
Un aggettivo si cambia in verbo coll'aggiunta delle terminazione *en*		
Si sopprime l'ausiliaro *do* per eccezione: dopo		

	Pagina	Esercizio
l'interrogativo *who* e coi verbi *to need* e *to dare*.	57	305
Si aggiunge l'ausiliare *do* per maggior forza, anche nelle frasi affermative	57	303
Quando due verbi al futuro sono accompagnati da voci di tempo il primo si volge al presente.	59	308
L'infinito italiano soggetto di una proposizione si volge in inglese o con l'infinito o col participio presente	67	314
Le espressioni *non è vero ? davvero !* si volgono coll'ausiliare espresso o sottinteso nella frase antecedente	66	312
Si adopera l'ausiliare *to be* col participio presente per esprimere un'azione che si è o si era in procinto di fare.	48	314
Maniera di rendere l'infinito italiano quando seguito dal verbo *fare* e dai verbi *to feel, to see* e *to hear*	69, 72	316, 320
Uso del passato definito e indefinito	78	322
Maniera di esprimere in inglese le frasi: *è un ora che, son due anni che, da un mese* ecc.	80	324
Volere (*Will*) come verbo principale.	82	326
Volere innanzi a un soggiuntivo italiano	ivi	ivi
Maniera di rendere i participi passati dei verbi difettivi	ivi	ivi
Tabella dei verbi che vogliono piuttosto essere seguiti dal participio presente che dall'infinito.	93	327

Avverbio.

Formazione dell'avverbio dall'aggettivo coll'aggiunta della terminazioni *ly y*	101	301
Posto dell'avverbio.	ivi	ivi
Tabella di avverbii.	ivi	ivi
Posto della negazione; nei verbi ausiliari si mette dopo il verbo	29	19
Una proposizione non può avere due negazioni.	106	82
No, not; quando si usa l'uno, quando l'altro.	ivi	ivi

Preposizioni.

Preposizione *a*; moto e riposo	18	7

— 231 —

	Pagina	Esercizio
Preposizioni *a*, *da* seguite da nome proprio o sostantivo personale o corrispondente al *chez* dei francesi	79	59
Proposizioni *di da* tra due sostantivi di cui uno indica la materia di cui l'altro è formato o l'uso a cui serve	229	179
Tabella di verbi seguiti da preposizioni	126	Il vol.
Maniera di esprimere le ore del giorno	147	117
Maniera di esprimere l'età	177	140
Maniere di rendere la particella *ne* secondo i suoi varii significati	307	221 e seg.
Signore, signora, signorina o signori	20, 60 121, 498	11, 41 91, 100

Fraseologia commerciale

Maniere di cominciare le lettere commerciali	463	385
» finire	464	ivi
Affari in generale	465	ivi
Nomenclatura di merci	466	ivi

INDICE DELLE LETTURE

che servono anche di esercizio di traduzione e conversazione

VOLUME I.

	Pag.
Philip the second	21
Darius king of Persia	33
Gracchus the husband of Cornelia	42
Early Rising	52
The danger of confiding in Strangers	63
The dog's will	74
Comparative honesty	83
Modesty of a youth	92
The Dream interpreted	101
The doctor who received the life of his patient in payment for his visits	109
Fiction and Truth	118
A pickpocket	121
The emperor Joseph	133
Honour	112
Ignorance mortified	151
Dignity maintd	160
Poverty of Epictetus	169
A curious decision	177
An astrologer and a king	190

The double lesson	199
The mysterious Englishmen	209
The advantage of not being able to swim	225
Fidelity	233
Before you promise calculate your ability to perform	241
Which is the king?	264
Alexander the Great	276
Woman's promise	293
A place	304
The wardrobe	317
A wolf and a lamb	327
A very singular excuse	338

VOLUME II.

The Egg of Columbus	14
The sagacious Indian	25
Desperate Patriotism	35
The Biter bit	41
Curious expedient	53
Mr. Johnson and Mrs. Thrale	63
Female Heroism	74
The Clear-sighted Blind man	78

Ingratitude and avarish punished . . . . Pag.	98	Virtue, man's true interest.	181
Filial love and modest Benevolence	108	The giant and dwarf.	182
		How to communicate bad news.	183
		An inheritance.	185
A dreadful Adventure. . . .	120	Mary Queen of Scots. . . .	188
Providential escape from assassination	137	The story of a disabled soldier.	190
		On lying.	194
The lost Child found. . . .	144	Character of Alfred	196
The philosopher outdone. . .	176	Advice to a young tradesman	197
Dean Swift advice respecting Servants.	177	Rivers and sir Harry (a dialogue)	200
A Golden Rule.	ivi	A travelling scene	202
How to become Learned . .	ivi	Economy	203
Dr. Watts.	ivi	Education	204
Abstraction	178	On the duties of the young .	205
The most Unhappy	ivi	Pleasures of Literature . . .	206
Knowledge and Ignorance . .	179	How to pop the question. . .	207
Taste and Knowldge. . . .	ivi	A palace in Abyssinia. . . .	211
Musical taste.	ivi	The storming of Front-de-	
Political prudence	180	Œuf's castle.	214
Devouring books.	ivi		

INDICE DEI DIALOGHI FAMIGLIARI
che si trovano solo nel primo volume

Primo dialogo di prima necessità . . . . Pag.	23	Sulle ore del giorno	154
		Sul freddo.	162
Secondo dialogo idem . . .	38	Prima di pranzo.	170
Terzo idem	43	Del coricarsi.	182
Quarto Idem	55	La posta.	192
Per chiedere un favore . . .	67	Sulle mode.	202
Con un calzolaio.	78	Per passare il tempo. . . .	228
Sulla lingua Inglese	85	Per andare al teatro. . . .	235
Sulla lezione	95	Della villeggiatura	245
Con un cappellaio.	103	Per chieder il permesso di uscire	267
Con un venditore di calze . .	112	Con un sarto.	277
Per chieder in prestito della carta.	120	Nel giardino.	295
		Per vestirsi	306
Per chiedere un appartamento in affitto.	126	In un caffè	319
Con un negoziante di tela . .	136	Col barbiere.	329
Sopra le stagioni.	144	Al ristoratore	341

INDICE DELL' EPISTOLARIO

	Pagina	Esercizio
Biglietto per pregare il maestro di non venire alla lezione	334	257
Per pregar un amico di trovar un impiego .	42	293
Per chieder il prezzo corrente con risposta .	61	307
Di un venditore al minuto a un mercante e risposta.	107	347
Per chieder imprestito libri durante malattia e risposta.	147	369
Modelli di biglietti, d'invito con risposta, per chiedere abboccamenti ecc.	161	384
Lettere commerciali	167 e seg.	386 e seg.

FINE

www.ingramcontent.com/pod-product-compliance
Lightning Source LLC
Chambersburg PA
CBHW020408230426
43664CB00009B/1233